AUTHENTIC HEARTS

Transform Your Relationships
Through Self-Love

TRUE AUTHENTICITY PRESS

LOHAN BRUGUERA

Authentic Hearts
2024 © Written by: Lohan Bruguera
2024 © Cover design by: Lohan Bruguera
2024 © Cover and all images by: Bing image Generator
2024 © Design by: Sambybooks
2024 © Editing by: Lynda McDaniels & DC Storyology
All rights reserved.

Published by: True Authenticity Press
Miami, FL, USA, 2024
https://linktr.ee/LohanBruguera

All rights reserved. This book contains material protected under the International and Federal Copyright Laws and Treaties. Any unauthorized reprint of this material is prohibited. No part of this book may be reproduced or transmitted in any form or by any means, electronic or mechanical, including photocopying, recording, or by any information storage and retrieval system, without written permission from the publisher.
The only exception is for brief quotations in printed reviews.

The name(s) of real person(s) have been changed to protect their identity. Any resemblance to actual persons, living or dead, or events, are purely coincidental and unintentional. We respect individual privacy and are committed to maintaining confidentiality.

Paperback ISBN: 979-8-9903892-0-5

Library of Congress Control Number: 2024906155

Printed in the United States of America
©2024 Lohan Bruguera and True Authenticity Press

TRUE AUTHENTICITY PRESS

Dedication

In loving memory of Maia Dhyan, February 1939 to October 2004

Foreword

Few things can take us to the heights of ecstasy and the depths of despair as quickly and as frequently as relationships. Few things knock us off balance as easily and disconcertingly. Few things capture our focus and consume our attention as completely. Entire industries exist for the purpose of enhancing the possibilities of love, sex, and relationships.

Love and relationships can make us feel as though we are on top of the world or plummet us into deepest doubt, darkest despair, and ruthless self-questioning, all in the space of seconds. They can make us hurt so bad that emotional pain becomes physical. There are interesting studies about a real heart problem called "Broken Heart Syndrome" that stems from loss, grief, and damaged relationships.

The more I interact with participants in retreats, workshops and other settings, the more evidence I find for the premise that most of us give our power away in the context of romantic relationships. This is where I consistently witness otherwise successful and empowered people selling out on their power, too often settling for a few crumbs of acceptance, validation, or pseudo-love. Otherwise, self-defined and strong-minded individuals, who are established professionally and even spiritually, can lose their sense of self when it comes to intimate relationships. They forfeit their power to avoid being alone, or for an illusory form of love.

Navigating relationships consciously is not easy. In fact, it's nothing short of heroic. Yet, when we do, our process of healing and transformation is sped up dramatically. And our relationships have an actual chance at success!

I have known Lohan Bruguera for over 30 years and can vouch for the authentic way in which he approaches life. That is also evident in his writing. He shares his hard-earned insights and perceptions generously. His commitment to helping others navigate the labyrinth of relationships is clear. It is also clear that he is willing to do the work it takes to have successful relationships. And that is nothing less than honorable.

I hope his book supports you to deepen your understanding of some of the reasons we experience such challenges around relationships. Yes, they require a lot of work, but approached consciously, they are well worth that effort. Blessings on your journey!

Christian de la Huerta,
Award-winning and Best-Selling Author of
Coming Out Spiritually: A Next Step
Awakening the Soul of Power: How to Live Heroically and Set Yourself Free

Personal Transformational Coach, Retreat Facilitator and Ted-X Speaker

Preface

Since my adolescence, I searched for that "something more". Something beyond a normal existence. After graduating high school, based on my observations of the adults who surrounded me and ill-prepared for what lay ahead, I knew, "There has to be more to Life than going to work, coming home, eating, TV and sleep, only to rinse and repeat." The thought of living that life never felt satisfying *for me*.

As a result, I was fascinated with self-help, meta-physics and spirituality—so I could understand what it meant to live a meaningful life and discover what I was missing. At nineteen, I became a staff member of a well-known yet controversial "self-help/spiritual" organization for about a year. The experience changed me in important ways. It gave me the ability to speak to anyone, about anything. My job, as a bookseller, was to approach strangers every day. It also left me traumatized by "spiritual" organizations. Although I gained a foundation of truthful teachings within myself, I abandoned my search for that elusive Life I wanted. Shortly after my twenty-seventh birthday, I awoke feverish, feeling miserable. I pulled out my thermometer from its thin plastic case, shook it vigorously and put the silver-colored tip under my tongue. My temperature was 102 °. I immediately took aspirin, but the effect only lasted a few hours before my fever rose again. Over the course of that day my physical state worsened, affecting my emotional state of being. I laid on the couch in a state of *numb-powerless*. The television was on, but very little attention was present. I was hungry but couldn't summon the energy to fix myself anything. I was so deep in my inert state that, although I felt empty and sad, a pervasive numbness was my primary experience. That night, everything changed. As if I was simply waiting to leave my body and physical reality. There was no fear involved. It was too high of a vibration emotionally for me to reach. I was merely waiting for some impending occurrence. Then, as thoughts drifted in and out of my mind, I thought about my parents—how grief-stricken they would be. I felt an intense sadness for them, *but not for myself*. I had no strength to resist my inevitable transition…and all I could do was to surrender. For five days, I lived this cycle of numbness and inevitability, where each day seemed to augment my experience. On the fifth night I had an epiphany. *"Wait a minute."* My inner voice—said, *"If I leave now, I'll have to come back and do this again, starting from zero. Before I leave, I want to get to the level that, if I come back, it's to help other people."*

The next day, my fever broke.

I gradually felt better, but the intense experience left me with a sense of urgency. It said, *"You don't have time to mess around anymore. Get on with it!"* I knew it was time to resume my search again. I devoured books about 'new age spirituality', in an attempt to satisfy this urgency that had ignited. I have since realized how important perceptions are, and how they form our experiences. Whether or not I was actually close to death, I had a near-death experience, with the same effects.

After a few months, a man at a party told me about a seminar called, "A Call to Greatness." I chose to attend. The creator and facilitator, Isana Mada, was a spiritual teacher who would become *my teacher and Guru*. She spoke to my soul so clearly and sharply that I could not deny the connection or underlying implications of our impending relationship. After a year and a half, I moved to San Francisco to live in an ashram (a spiritual community) with her and three other disciples (students) for two years. We apprenticed in breathwork and practiced her teachings, based on authentic Self-expression. Eventually, she gave us her body of work and empowered us to become teachers and healers. Most importantly, she provided practical tools to connect with and express our true Selves. She helped us see our own egoic tendencies that sabotaged our spiritual growth and gave us clear guidance to help us transcend them.

I had the privilege of being in close relationship with Isana Mada for more than fourteen years, until her passing.

Although I have been able to process my Life and experiences through her teachings, it is only these last few years that the teachings descended from my head to my heart. That transition has enabled me to naturally live the teachings, rather than processing my Life through them, after the fact. It is from this deepening that this book has come into being. May it help illuminate your way, and further your journey to authentic Self-expression.

Lohan

Note to The Reader

My intention is to impart teachings that help YOU participate in relationships with a higher level of awareness. My wish is that it will broaden your perspective; help your relationships; and contribute to a deeper sense of personal freedom.

Throughout the book, I share stories from my own life, as well as fictionalized stories to illustrate a point. I happen to be a gay man, therefore most of my stories involve two men. They are not meant to challenge anyone's principles or beliefs, and if you prefer the stories reflect yours, then feel free to change the name or names as you read. I would ask that you not allow any preference to override the teachings that can make a difference in your relationships and Life.

Well into my twenties, I hid who I am, sensitive to other people's beliefs about right and wrong, and adjusting my authentic nature to be accepted by society. Even though preferences are only a small part of who we are, we should not require anyone to hide any part of themselves to be accepted.

This work is an authentic expression that wrote itself through me, and as such, I will not change, adjust or adapt it for anyone else's thoughts or beliefs. That is what got us into trouble and keeps us from becoming our true Selves.

Acknowledgements

I am grateful for the people who have come into my Life, for a minute, an hour, a season or a Lifetime to assist each other in this journey toward enlightenment. Everyone who enters our lives enters for that purpose, whether we are aware of it or not.

I also want to give special thanks to those souls who are closest to me who have allowed me a space to practice my most authentic-Self and have been with me through this process. Without their presence in my Life, I surely would be lost.

Most importantly, not a day goes by in which I don't feel the impact of my spiritual teacher's presence. Even though it has been close to twenty years since her departure, I feel her with me every day. It is very rare, indeed, on this most confusing, complicated and diverse planet, to find another soul around whom you feel fully safe to be your most vulnerable Self and know, at the deepest level, that your highest good for spiritual evolution is being served by them. Isana Mada Grace Dhyana, (later known as Maia Dhyan at the time of her passing), was that one other soul for me in this Lifetime. She assisted me in creating my own personal relationship and path to God and never presumed to be the one through which that connection existed. So my greatest thanks and gratitude go to Maia and what she represents in my Life, my conscious evolution and my personal connection to God.

Introduction

I wrote this book with romantic relationships in mind, but these teachings and practices will work for any personal relationship. However, these teachings will only work upon a foundation of commitment and desire.

1.Commitment

Both people need to commit to becoming more conscious. You cannot do the work of personal growth for anyone else. It is vital that you communicate with your partner, friend or family member and make an agreement with each other that you will both commit to make the changes that Self-awareness demands. Revisiting that agreement occasionally is also important, to remind each other that you are on the same team and are still willing to follow through on that commitment.

2.Desire

Both people need to *want* to be in—and *work* on—their relationship. This mostly happens with family members with whom we feel an obligation to be in relationship, but not necessarily the desire. These teachings will not work to make this type of relationship clearer. Do the best you can, but do not expect much.

I came to understand this as a result of failing to employ the teachings in a particular relationship. This was a difficult realization for me, and it brought me much sadness, but at the time I had to admit to myself that I was not really interested in having a relationship with them. It did give me the clarity, however, as to why I was unable to practice the teachings in this case. In these types of relationships, we will find many opportunities to express our truth, and it is possible that our feelings toward them may change. If we continue with our commitment to be the truth of ourselves and come from a transparent, open place in relating with them, we may heal the issues in the process and recreate the relationship.

Remember, we all have the right to make our own choices as long as they do not include harming others. Being authentic will never include this. None of us is obligated to be in or work on any relationship. That is totally our choice.

I hope you find the information and practices in this book helpful and applicable in your Life. Also, remember that our capacity for understanding changes over time, and if you choose to reread this text, you will probably pick up on things that you did not absorb from your previous read.

I wish you a wonderful journey of Self. The hero's journey.

CONTENTS

Dedication
Foreword
Preface
Note to the Reader
Acknowledgements
Introduction

Chapter 1:   Our Book of Life is Blank

Chapter 2:   The Experience Quotient—Changing our Perceptions

Chapter 3:   Resentment is a Bad Word

Chapter 4:   Everybody Loves a Honeymoon

Chapter 5:   Team Ego Plays Defense

Chapter 6:   Communication—A Powerful Gift

Chapter 7:   Keeping Secrets and Lies, Oh My!

Chapter 8:   You Hold My Space and I'll Hold Yours

Chapter 9:   Our Minds Doing Algebra—Solving The X-Factor

Chapter 10:   Can You Get to Gratitude?

Chapter 11:   I'll Never Do That Again—Life's Lessons

Chapter 12:   Free And Clear Spaces—The How-To's

Chapter 13:   Divine What? Spiritual Who?

Appendix
About the Author

Appendix
About the Author

CONTENTS

Dedication
Foreword
Preface
Note to the Reader
Acknowledgements
Introduction
Chapter 1:   Our Book of Life is Blank

Chapter 2:   The Experience Quotient—Changing our Perceptions

Chapter 3:   Resentment is a Bad Word

Chapter 4:   Everybody Loves a Honeymoon

Chapter 5:   Team Ego Plays Defense

Chapter 6:   Communication—A Powerful Gift

Chapter 7:   Keeping Secrets and Lies, Oh My!

Chapter 8:   You Hold My Space and I'll Hold Yours

Chapter 9:   Our Minds Doing Algebra—Solving The X-Factor

Chapter 10:   Can You Get to Gratitude?

Chapter 11:   I'll Never Do That Again—Life's Lessons

Chapter 12:   Free And Clear Spaces—The How-To's

Chapter 13:   Divine What? Spiritual Who?

Chapter 1

Our Book of Life Is Blank

Experts agree that from the time we are born until about seven we are all in a semi-hypnotic state. Part of us is participating with the events Life presents to us and part of us is in "observer mode", learning how to operate in a strange world we find ourselves in. In this semi-hypnotic state, everything is observed and recorded by the subconscious mind.

Most of us are brought forth by parents who have not been taught how to effectively communicate. They were never shown how to process and express their emotions, how to be an authentic expression of their inner-selves; or how to maintain and do the work for functional relationships. Let's face it, these are topics that have not been historically addressed at all. We are all left to learn these most basic skills of Life on our own. Some people do well, and others fall short.

As a result, a great majority of us have been exposed to many traumatic experiences in our childhood, which lead to negative conditioning that affects our view of Life. Remember too, that as children we do not have the tools or capacity to process what is happening in an informed or conscious way. If Daddy is not around, we feel abandoned. We cannot rationalize that Daddy has to work so we can eat. We cannot understand that Daddy is loving and taking care of us. We think that Daddy is not around because Daddy does not *Love* us. We believe we must *not be worthy of Love*. And, if God forbid, Mommy and Daddy split up, a child thinks: *Daddy left me. He does not Love me. I must not be worthy of Love.*

So, it's not only the negative experiences, but also the *perceived* negative experiences that begin to write themselves on our Life pages. More than likely, we have many pleasant and happy experiences as well. Let's not forget those. We carry them all with us. In fact, every moment of our lives is stored in our database of memory. This is how our first chapters are written in our own Book of Life. But until we start to identify the difference between how we *truly* feel and our *learned* ideals and behaviors, we will unconsciously revert to those first chapters, and they will be a frame of reference for our attitudes, choices and actions.

> "So, it's not only the negative experiences, but also the perceived negative experiences that begin to write themselves on our Life pages."

I'll give you an example. When I was nineteen, I dated Diego for a few months. We got together mostly on the weekends. We disagreed very seldom, and our relationship was mostly loving and affectionate. When we did have the occasional disagreement, we resolved it relatively quickly. At some point in the relationship, Diego started to not follow through on the plans we had made. After this happened a few times, I took it as a sign that he was no longer interested in continuing our relationship, and I got us together to resolve things. I told him that I thought we should no longer see each other. He asked me why. I answered, "It's what you are demonstrating you want by standing me up and not keeping our plans." His response was so insignificant, so uncaring that I cannot remember what he said. I ended our relationship then and there. Not without feeling the sadness and the loss of this man in my Life, but that is another story.

The amazing thing is that about fourteen years later I happened to bump into Diego at a restaurant where he worked. I was really happy to see him and wanted to know about the huge blank space since we last saw each other. I invited him to my apartment after his shift to catch up and I would make him dinner. He accepted. We passed the time telling each other about the paths our Life journeys had taken us. Both of our lives had directed us through turn-filled, indirect routes that no GPS could have predicted or suggested. I felt very happy to know about him, and I could feel the same from him.

At one point he asked me, "Do you know why we broke up?"
"Why?" I asked.

"I was raised in a very conflictive environment; my family was always fighting and arguing. I thought it was how relationships were supposed to be. You never fought with me, so I thought that you didn't Love me."

That night I fully grasped how much our upbringing shades the way we perceive things.

> *We filter our reality through shades of previous observations and conclusions. Mostly formed up to the age of seven. These foundational experiences become the primary links of similar chains of experiences.*

I had almost the opposite upbringing. My parents never argued in front of us. In fact, I remember my parents speaking in serious tones only once. I was probably nine or ten, sitting in the back seat of the car and feeling very sad, crying quietly because I could tell they were not happy with each other. I was so unused to them not being loving to one another. As nice as that sounds, I now realize I was deprived of learning early on about healthy conflict resolution.

Once we learn something, it is stored in the subconscious mind, and we do not have to learn it again. This is how sports work. Let's take volleyball. We do drills until they are second nature. Bump. Set. Spike. We practice different plays— defensive and offensive. And then, practice, practice, practice until the plays become part of our body's memory, stored in our subconscious. Once we learn the basic techniques, we don't have to think about what to do. We become as present with the ball and respond to it with the best our body can muster. (We do our best to get to the ball.) The rest is taken care of. If I had to stop to think how many elements are involved in spiking a volleyball over the net, the game would grind to a halt as I considered where the ball is set, how the wind will move it, how best to make my approach, when to jump, how I will hit the ball— as it is coming down? Where to direct the ball (aim) and many more details that my subconscious mind processes in a split second.

It works much the same with our book of Life. The first chapters have given us a template, and as we move through our lives using that template, we repeat behaviors, attitudes, addictions, and choices that carve deep grooves in ourselves. That is why it is difficult to not fall into old patterns, because it is as if gravity slides us into those grooves without permission or awareness. This is why becoming more conscious in our lives requires practice. Sometimes we slip into those grooves and have to clean up the mess again. But as we practice, we will get better and better, and sometimes have the welcomed realization that we didn't slip even though we were right on the edge.

So yes, we start with blank pages, and they are quickly written as our Life unfolds. But those pages are not written with indelible ink. We can edit and change our learned, unconscious patterns by making the unconscious conscious. This takes courage, determination, and a willingness to be brutally honest in our Self-reflection. Our commitment to that choice will be carried inside of our being.

In the meantime, remember to forgive yourself for imperfections. Treat yourself with Love and kindness. Comfort yourself when you fall short, take responsibility by doing damage control and always strive to do better next time.

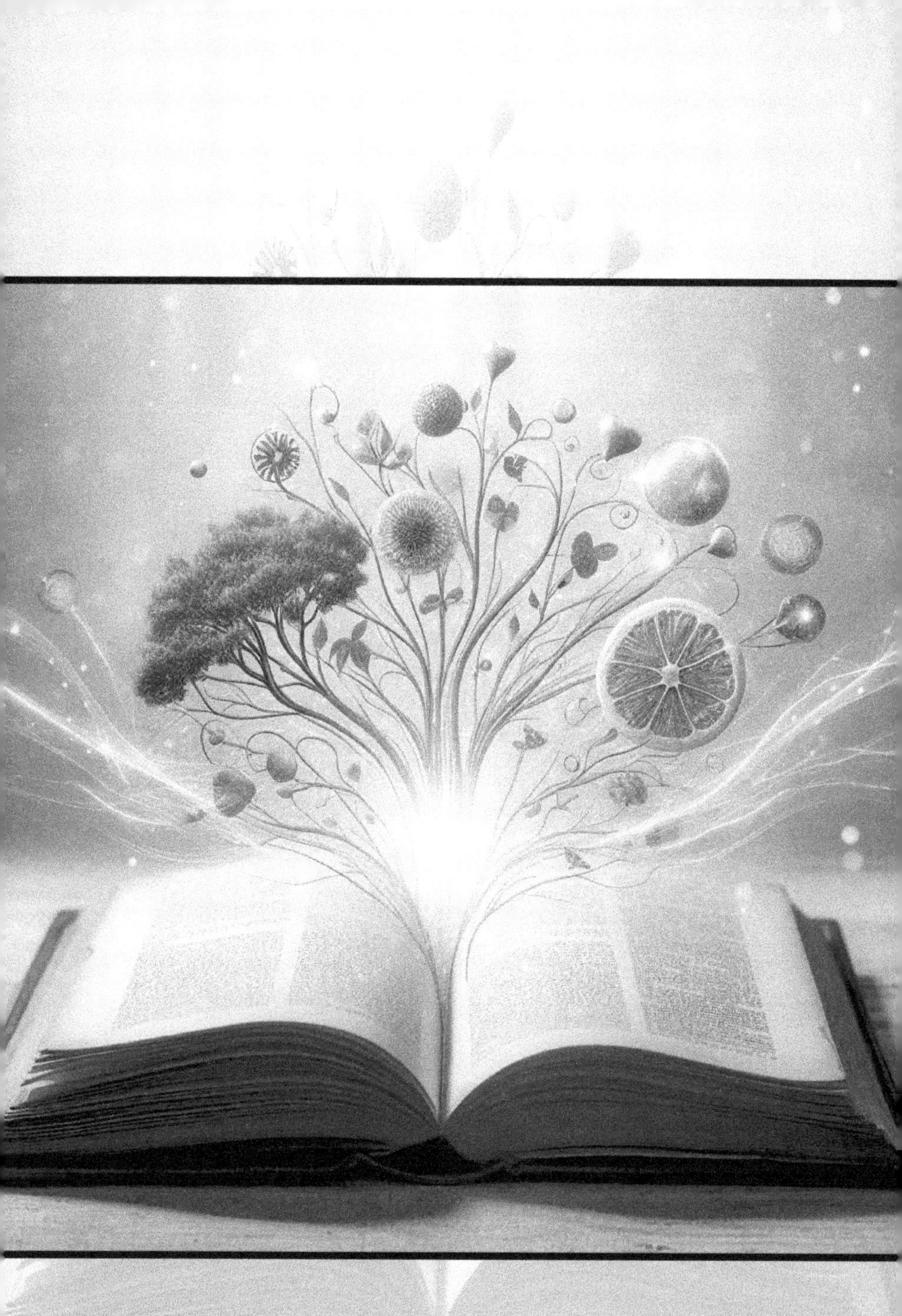

Chapter 2

The Experience Quotient—Changing Our Perceptions

How are our experiences created and formed? From my perspective, experiences are .001% content and 99.99% perception. Content is the actual happenings of the experience and perception is how we filter, view, or interpret the content. So, in essence, our perception is what creates our experience.

> **Paul**, **Susan**, **Kyle**, and **Brad** are trapped in an elevator in the dark, in between floors for two hours. The "content" is the same for all four people. They are trapped in an elevator in the dark, in between floors for two hours.
>
> <u>Paul</u> is claustrophobic, which causes varying degrees of panic in the form of high fear and anxiety. This will cause him to have a very traumatic experience.
>
> <u>Susan</u> missed her morning meditation and is taking the time now to meditate and center herself. This will help her create a peaceful experience.
>
> <u>Kyle</u> is on his way to attend an important business

meeting, and his presence there could determine the success of the financial venture the meeting pertains to. This situation could cause him to be late and maybe even miss this important meeting altogether. To top it off, his cell phone has no reception in the elevator, and he cannot contact his boss to let him know what is happening. This will likely create an anxious, uncertain experience with a high level of frustration.

Brad does not have anywhere he has to be. He was going jogging but feels bored and has feelings of not making full use of his time. Which could create a meaningless, empty experience.

As you can see, each person's perception of *what* is happening is creating their experience.

Can we actually change how we perceive a happening in order to change our experience? The answer is yes! We can use our inner dialog, which tries to make sense and maybe even see the bigger picture to change our perception—and change our experience.

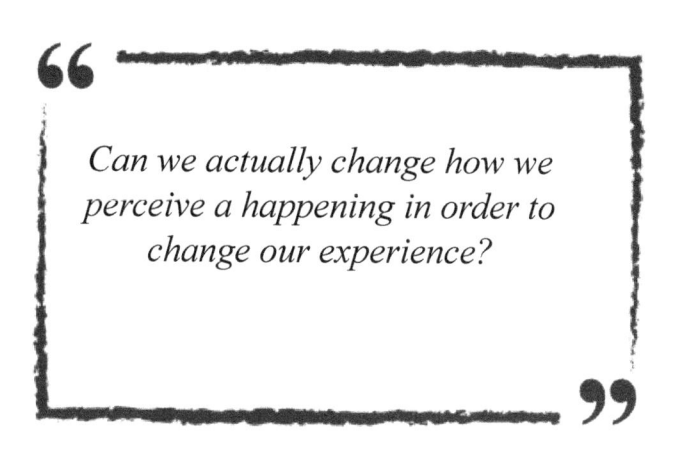

> *Can we actually change how we perceive a happening in order to change our experience?*

If we do not make a conscious choice in our perception, this choice will be determined by our subconscious. Perhaps negative past experiences will be triggered that could be painful and elicit a negative reaction ranging from mild to extreme. Or we may have no negative experiences triggered at all.

In this true story, Jason and Matt met each other on a coolOctober night. They chatted on a dating app, had a long phone conversation, and then decided to meet in person. After a month of very intense dating, romance, and intimacy, it was obvious to both that this would be a significant relationship. Matt was riding his bike from a friend's house one evening when his pant leg got caught in the chain and threw him off balance. When he fell, his right big toe hit the curb hard and caused a clean fracture through the bone.

The point to this story is two-fold.

>**1.** That we may draw an initial conclusion or judgment based on what we have experienced or how we perceive a situation. Later, though, we may change the way we see the situation as a result of how it unfolds.
>
>**2.** That it is totally possible to change our perception and, as a result, change our experience. In that conversation, Jason offered Matt a different way to look at the reality of his Life. Matt could have chosen to remain stuck in his perception; only he could make the choice to change. He accepted the way Jason was able to view it and even accepted that Jason took the burden of the expenses to facilitate this possibility.

Is there any circumstance in your Life that you are dissatisfied with? If so, ask yourself what would be a broader, more expanded way of looking at this. Notice if your mind is set and unyielding. If it is, just live in the question and see if something occurs to you when you least expect it. Remember, there are countless ways to view any reality.

Try this effective practice: Take a circumstance, real or imagined, and view it as if you were different people with different mindsets and different agendas. Challenge yourself to see how flexible you can be mentally and how many different viewpoints you can come up with. You can even make a game of it and play it with your friends. It's fun!

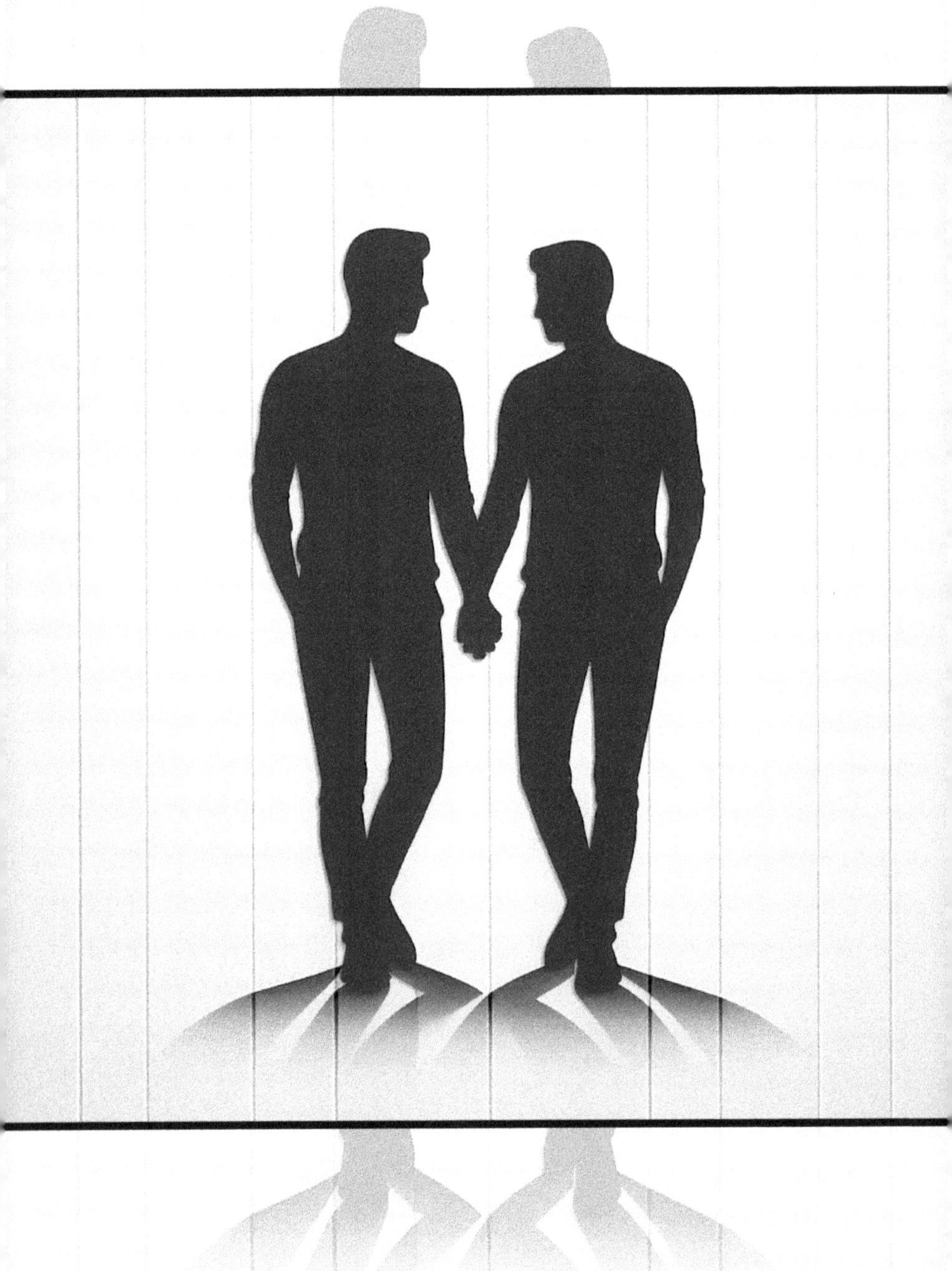

Chapter 3

Resentment Is a BAD Word!!

In order to understand resentments, we must also talk about its close cousin: disappointment. Although we may experience them independent of one another, many times they walk the pathways of our psyche hand in hand. They can certainly cause us to feel similar emotions.

*"Disappointment is the **negative emotion you feel when an outcome doesn't match up to your expectations**. Characterized by feelings of **sadness, loss, anger, and frustration….**"* (mensline.org.au, September 2023 https://mensline.org.au/how-to-deal-with-anger/how-to-deal-with-disappointment/)

*"Resentment describes a **negative emotional reaction to being mistreated**. There is no one cause of resentment, but most cases involve an underlying sense of being mistreated or wronged by another person."* (webmd.com, September 2023 https://www.webmd.com/mental-health/signs-resentment)

How do disappointment and resentment show up in relationships? Most of us bring many expectations to our relationships, and most of these expectations are determined by what we need and want from the other. In other words, how our partner "should" behave. Let's be real—nobody goes into a relationship without wanting or needing something. Even simple companionship will come with our unique set of parameters and conditions. Most of these are determined by how we downloaded our programing on "how to do Life," which started when we were born until around seven. If we have done extensive work on ourselves, our expectations might be considerably less.

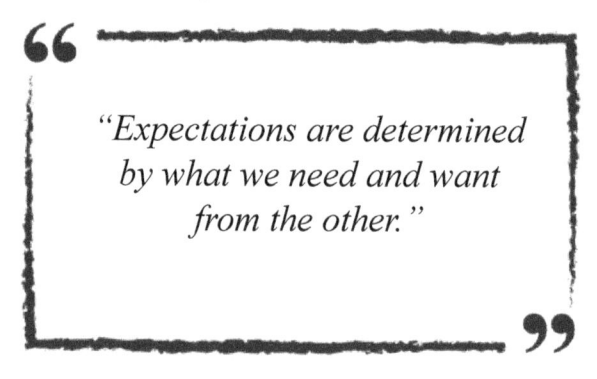

> *"Expectations are determined by what we need and want from the other."*

So, let's say that in our relationship, one of our expectations is not being met. For example, we feel the need to have constant validation from our partner. This causes us a degree of disappointment, which will be accompanied by some kind of emotional experience. Our disappointment is caused by expectations that are, in all likelihood, colored by our past and how we perceive things "*should*" be. Because our perception is what determines our experience, we need to realize that *often* we are having an emotional reaction to not only what is actually happening in the present moment but to previous similar experiences. The emotional energy from these past experiences was likely never released by acting and responding in an authentic, honest and vulnerable way. As a result, this energy actually has an amplifying effect on the present-day situation.

> "Our disappointment is caused by expectations that are, in all likelihood, colored by our past and how we perceive things "should" be... often we are having an emotional reaction to not only what is actually happening in the present moment but to previous similar experiences"

If, on the other hand, we have done extensive work on ourselves and process ourselves so that we take responsibility for our own feelings, thoughts, and emotions, we primarily feel the emotions related to not having our expectations met in the *present-day experience*. In which case we are able to direct less blame toward our partner for our unfulfilled expectations. This Self-processing will also help us to decipher what we need to communicate, if anything, to release the emotions that do come up.

When we do *not* take responsibility for our emotional reactions and blame the other person because they did not meet our expectations, resentment is certain to follow. If we cling to the perception that our expectations of our partner are realistic and valid, we will also have the perception of being mistreated or wronged by that other person. And here comes resentment again.

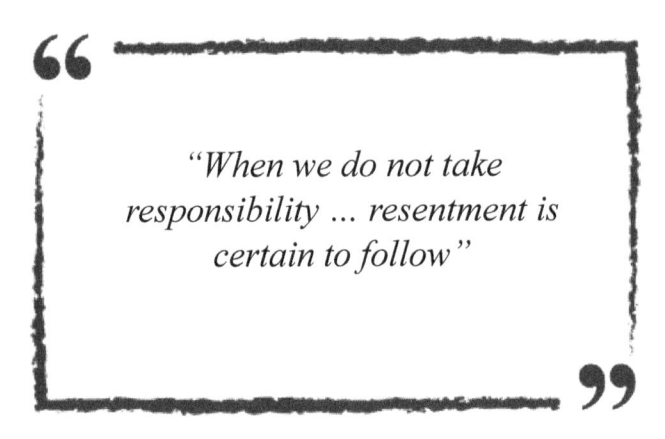

> *"When we do not take responsibility ... resentment is certain to follow"*

Interestingly, we don't actually have to be mistreated to *feel* as though we are *being* mistreated. If we perceive mistreatment, we will experience mistreatment. So, it is very important when relating to another person to have a conscious measure of how much blame we are placing on *them* for *our* disappointment. And keep in mind that that degree of blame will deliver the same degree of resentment.

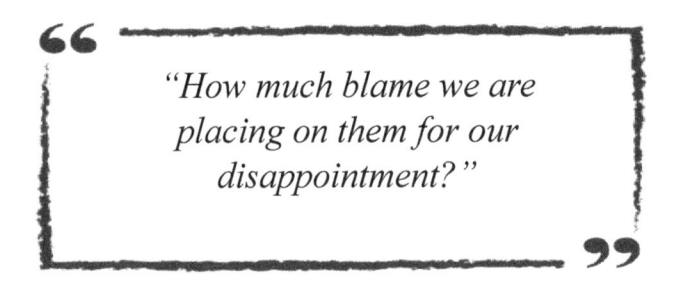

> *"How much blame we are placing on them for our disappointment?"*

Many of us think of resentment as a bad word, something that we should not feel or are wrong to feel. Resentment, however, is a natural part of being disappointed if we also feel any amount of blame toward someone for that disappointment. Resentment is *not* a bad word, nor are we bad people because we have resentments. Most of us walk around with a great degree of unconscious resentment. And if we realize that we've labeled resentment as a *bad* word, we probably have more roiling underneath than we can imagine. This happens because we never allowed ourselves to accept that we are capable of resentments, which makes them impossible to clear.

It is extremely important in a relationship to not let resentments accumulate. In the early days, we are often so overcome with Love that we feel our resentments are too small and too unimportant to give them voice. Also, we are sometimes afraid of risking the relationship or causing an upset. But don't kid yourself. The true risk is holding on to the small resentments and letting them grow. They will build up as surely as dust builds up on your furniture. And if this goes on long enough, no amount of furniture polish will be able to wipe it off. They will be so difficult to identify individually that you'll need to scrape them off in big sections of similar sticky resentments. It is so much easier to do the work from the beginning.

> *"The true risk is holding on to the small resentments and letting them grow."*

Please know this: the more resentments we build, the less space or capacity for Love we have for the person we hold those resentments against. Once we are able to voice our resentments, taking as much responsibility for our feelings, thoughts and emotions as we can and clearing them, we will once again feel Love for and connection to our partner.

Of course, we are not working on our resentments in a vacuum. When we are clearing our resentments, we need to keep in mind that we may say things in a way that will trigger our partner's unresolved past. Relationships have a way of connecting us with the old baggage of our past. We have all accumulated numerous check-ins and quite a few carry ons. So we will inadvertently pull something out of our partners suitcase. It will probably be something unwashed and smelly. Be prepared for this. Make an agreement with each other that you will do the work of maintaining a clean space and keeping it dust free.

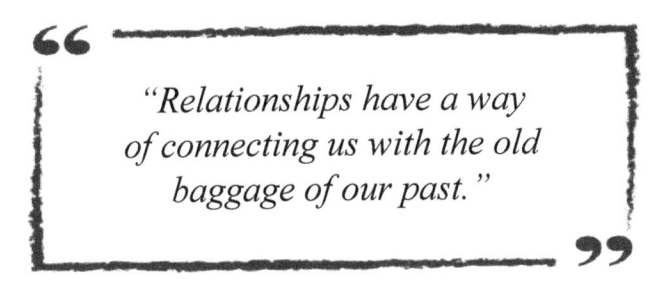

> "Relationships have a way of connecting us with the old baggage of our past."

We will go over clearing the space in another chapter. This chapter is intended to help us accept that all of us are capable of creating and holding on to resentments. If we have any kind of an all-but-perfect emotional past, we will be triggered and we will blame others until we do not. It takes a megaton of practice and until we are one hundred percent clear, we are all still in the process of clearing. So please accept that resentment may not be a pleasant word, but it is not a bad one. Give yourself permission to have your resentments, clear them and get back to Love as soon as possible.

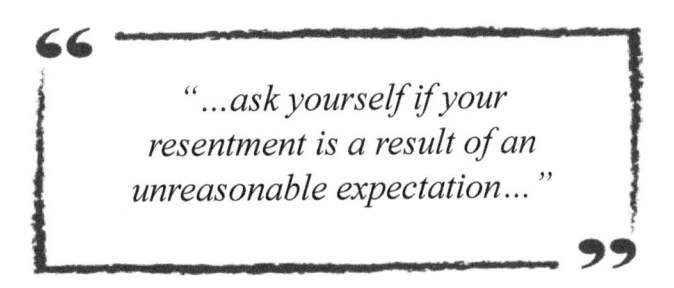

> "...ask yourself if your resentment is a result of an unreasonable expectation..."

Are you aware of any resentments you are holding against anyone in your Life? The first step after identifying a resentment is to ask yourself if it is a result of an unreasonable expectation. If so, it will naturally clear by way of this realization. If not, would it be possible to clear these resentments with them in open dialogue? Make a list of any resentments you may be holding on to, and after reading the chapter on clearing the space, attempt to agree to a clearing with each person. Do this with as much information as possible so the person does not feel blindsided. Do your best to take responsibility for your feelings and perceptions. Keep awareness on how much Love you hold toward this person before and after the clearing in order to gauge any changes.

How soon can we get back to Love? That is the real test.

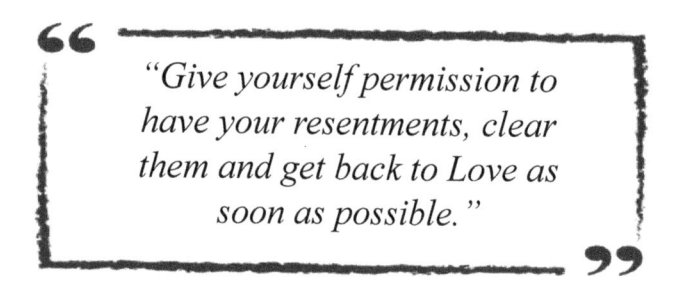

> *"Give yourself permission to have your resentments, clear them and get back to Love as soon as possible."*

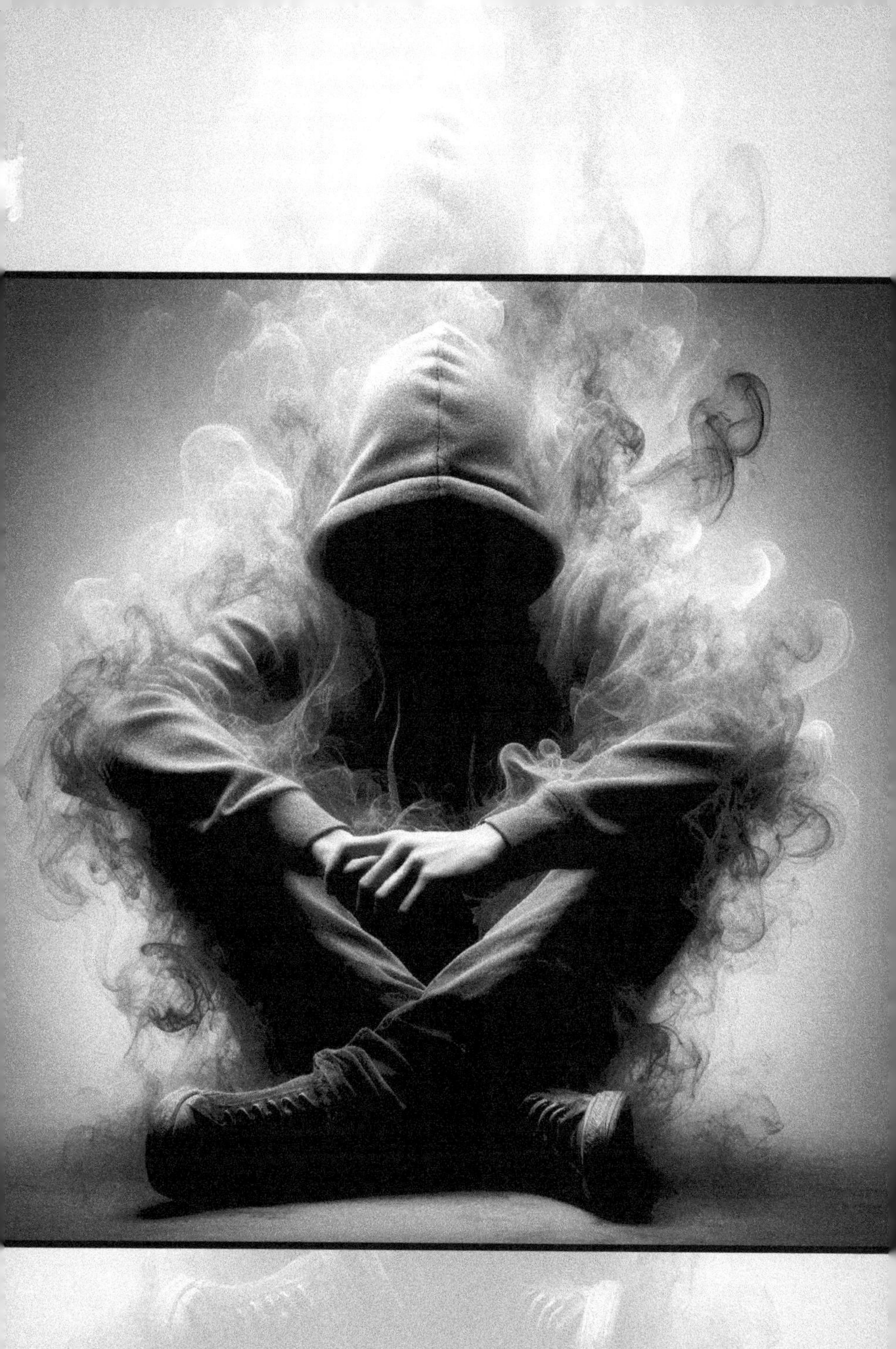

Chapter 4

Everybody Loves a Honeymoon

On this planet of almost eight billion people, it seems impossible that anyone could ever feel alone, and yet recent reports tell us loneliness is widespread. Also, as far as we know, there has never been a time in our history when happenings on the other side of the planet are instantly available for our viewing. We have unlimited knowledge at our fingertips and a multitude of platforms to share our thoughts, feelings, and viewpoints. So how could it be that anyone could feel isolated and separate?

To answer that, let's start by exploring the function of our egos. The ego is a necessary part of our ability to exist and operate in this physical reality. The ego is our intrinsic personality. It provides us with our unique, individual expression in this world. The function of the ego is to give us a separate sense of Self. Without the Ego we would be unable to express our personal stamp on the Self that radiates into this physical Life.

I like to use an analogy of our egos being jewels of different sizes, shapes and colors, and our higher Selves or our spirit Selves being the light of the Sun. When we hold these light transducing structures up to the illumination of the Sun, we will see different projections of light shining through them. Each one will have a different color, intensity, and pattern. Our spiritual light, the part of us that exists outside the physical reality, is connected to the All. This light shines through our ego, which is our unique jewel, and it projects this light into our physical plane. No other being possesses the same exact jewel as ours. It's the spiritual fingerprint that we leave on the surfaces of this reality.

> *"No other being possesses the same exact jewel as ours. It's the spiritual fingerprint that we leave on the surfaces of this reality."*

Now let's add another element to this. Because we all receive some level of psychological damage in our formative years, our jewel is also damaged. It gets scratched, smudged, occluded, and cracked. These flaws are also unique to us because no other person has gone through the exact experiences that we have or filtered them in the same way. The imperfections we have acquired throughout our lives distort, block, and diminish the light that would otherwise shine clearly through our jewel.

The real problem, however, is that we think that we are our

ego. We identify ourselves with our ego instead of it being solely an instrument of expression. Since our connection to our light is distorted by our trauma and since the function of the ego is to have a sense of individual Self, a separate identity, we feel isolated and alone. We identify so absolutely with our damaged self that we are unable to feel ourselves as more than that damage.

Our damaged ego is made up of our past conditioning and unresolved painful experiences, perceived or real. And our ego is always trying to protect itself from future painful experiences, so it reacts fearfully to that possibility. It is made up of unconscious protections, blocks and defenses that are very difficult for others to get through. They can show up as strong attitudes, expectations, judgments and demands. Isana Mada Grace Dhyana's model of the damaged ego in her book *"A Call to Greatness—A Spiritual Journey of Self-Discovery and Self-Expression—The Teachings of a Course In Congruence" Published by, Dhyana Press, Copyright Isana Mada 1994, page 208*, states, *"The ego has clear eyes into the past and dim vision in the present. It has a big noisy mouth, constantly chattering but with poor impaired hearing."* The ego mind has an accumulation of unconscious pain and trauma from our past, and we never know how or what will be triggered and cause us to react.

> *Any element in our present life can trigger unconscious pain and trauma from our past. It can be as simple as, a word, a look, an attitude, a sound, or smell.*

Of course, we are all on a spectrum of identification with our damaged ego. We have had moments of connection to something more, something bigger than the limitations we have experienced. Some of these moments are fleeting and some are longer lasting, but they all stir a yearning for more connection. We all want to feel less separate, less alone and to feel those moments when we are sharing ourselves with others of like resonance.

When we do find someone we feel a special connection to, we are swept into the experience of falling in Love and enter into the "Honeymoon Stage" of a relationship. Our feeling of connection to and Love for the other is so strong that our individual sense of Self becomes translucent. The membranethat separates us from each other becomes more porous and we meld into the space we create with one another. Our ego boundaries are temporarily disabled, to some degree. Time shifts. We feel physically energized and more expanded, connected, and enlightened than our normal state of being. It's intoxicating, which is why so many of us are addicted to this initial stage of a Love relationship. The trouble is, when it starts to wear off, we crave that falling-in-Love experience once again and go searching for the next ego-freedom high.

Since nothing lasts forever, this honeymoon phase will, at some point, start to diminish. As this occurs, the little things our partner does that were somehow cute and quirky transform into the not-so-little things that are now irritating and weird. This stage is where the real work of a relationship comes into play. This is when we need to realize that the irritation and weirdness is really just a trigger for our true-Self to clear unresolved negative emotional energies from *our* past. When we allow the past hurts of the ego to drive us to reactivity, we are not able to release the emotional energy of the trigger. Only by authentic expression are we able to release the emotional energy, not only of the present moment, but also of past similar experiences when we couldn't or didn't express ourselves authentically. By this I mean that we acknowledge what we are feeling and communicate it in a way that we can be heard. Not through automatic reactive attack or defense, but by expressing our true feelings and owning them. This takes courage and a willingness to put our neck on the chopping block of vulnerability.

> "...irritation and weirdness are really just a trigger for our true-Self to clear unresolved negative emotional energies."

If we look closely at this practice, though, we find its blessing. We see that it is a gift. We realize that being triggered is, in itself, an opportunity to clear our past. Once we are willing to be Self-reflective in an honest way, we will start healing the flaws of our jewel and our light will shine truer and brighter.

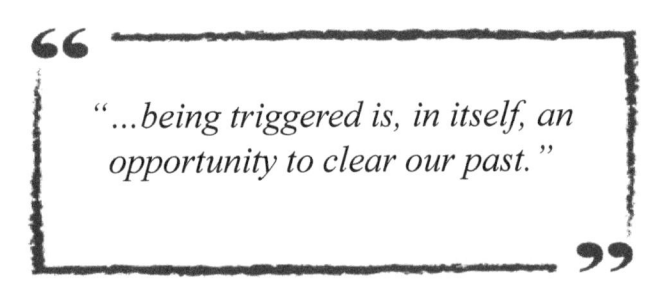

> "...being triggered is, in itself, an opportunity to clear our past."

We are all serving each other by triggering one another, which gives us opportunities to evolve and become more conscious. Let's make one thing very clear. You may not want to hear this, but that won't make it any less true. As long as we blame anything or anyone outside of ourselves for something, we are powerless to change it. We have no power to change anyone else or to control how others behave or respond. We can only change ourselves. So, if we are confronted with something that causes us to feel discomfort or triggers an emotional reaction, that is when we look inside ourselves to decipher what it is we need to express. We always need to take responsibility for our own feelings and emotions, even when others are acting awful and inappropriate. After all, who else is having our experiences but us? Everyone is having their own set of experiences that form their individual lives. We have a choice only when it comes to our own.

Once we truly grasp the lesson from a particular experience, we will probably notice that we no longer attract this type of experience to our Life. And, even if we do, it will not affect us the way it had. We may even be surprised by our own equanimity in the face of a prior trigger. If, on the other hand, we are constantly attracting the same type of people and experiences to our reality, then it's time to do our best to grow from them, so that we can move on to the next lesson.

If you experience a persistent situation you cannot change that is causing you emotional distress, ask yourself this: How can I choose to perceive this in a way that will cause me less distress? There are unlimited ways in which to view a situation. And depending on how we look at something, our experience of it will change.

Everybody Loves a honeymoon, but if we are only willing to

live in the honeymoon suite, we are not taking full advantage of the opportunities intrinsic to our unconscious past coming to the surface. All of this is coming up in order to heal, because our past really wants to be healed.

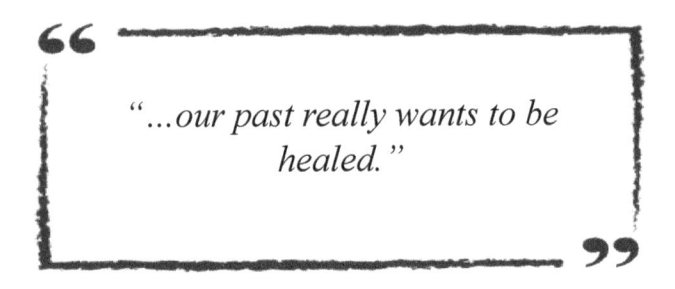

> *"...our past really wants to be healed."*

Do you remember when you had an emotional upset and realized in retrospect that you over reacted? This is an example of your damaged ego being triggered and reacting with the added force of your past trauma and pain. Sometimes it can take a long time to recover from this imbalance. Other times it is faster. Begin to notice how much time it takes you to return to your balanced Self and do your best to shorten that time. How much time have we all wasted being consumed with and perpetuating our reactivity?

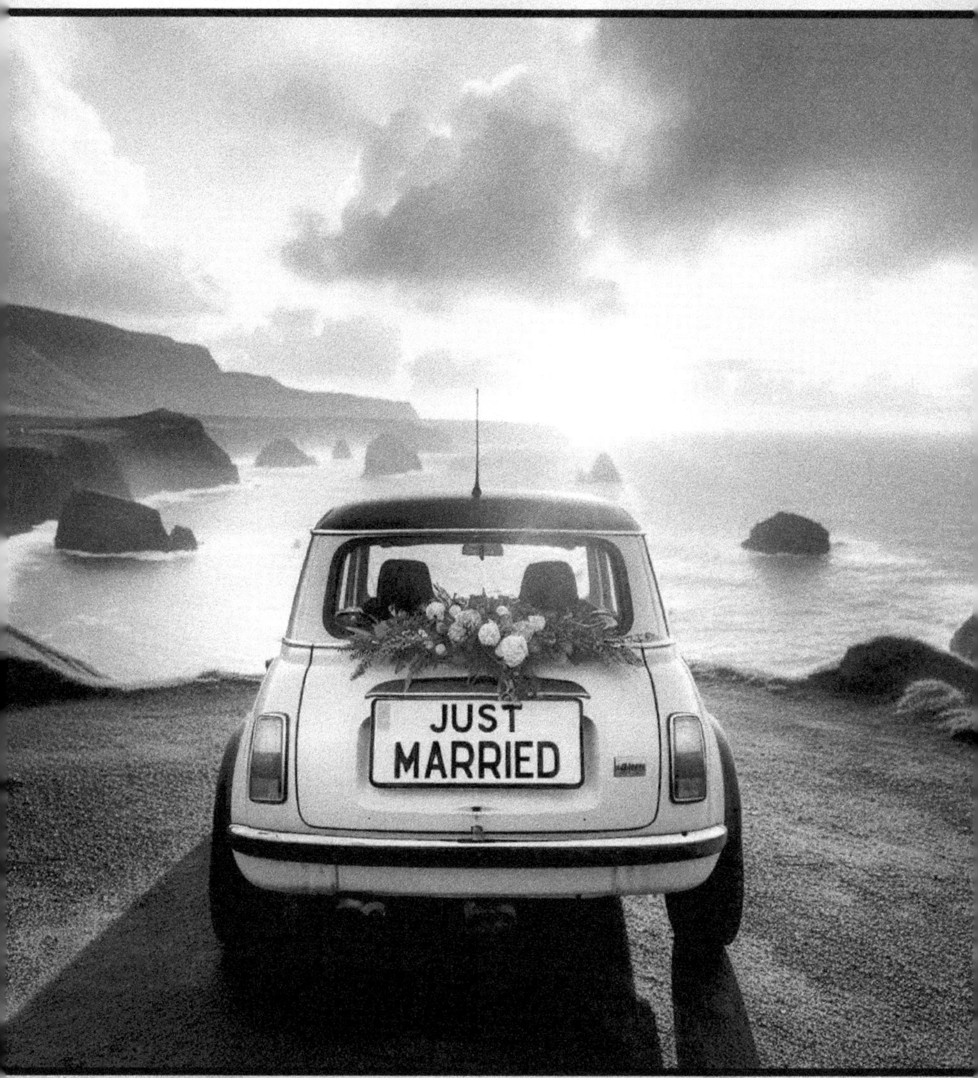
JUST
MARRIED

Chapter 5

Team Ego Plays Defense

Now I'd like to dig deeper into how the Ego maintains itself as the main player in our lives.

Remember how our ego jewel has gotten scratched, smudged, occluded, and cracked? Well, any time one of these flaws is activated, it is usually associated with pain. Most of us would agree that we are naturally open to pleasure and would prefer to not experience pain. As a result, our fragile ego automatically goes into defensive mode on the playing field of our lives, watching out for and trying to avoid pain. This happens any time our fragile ego perceives a possible threat.

When we are young and still in the minor leagues, our defenses are more obvious. Someone calls us a name and we say "Nuh-uh, you're a (fill in the blank)." However, once we are drafted into the majors, our repertoire of reactions becomes less apparent and more subtle. We have lived a childhood of practicing the defensive arts and have become experts in defensive strategies that help us hide the truth.

Some basic defense tactics we have in our armory: denial, justifications or reasons, blame, passive/aggressive, victim or combative, conflictive, critical, and attack or intimidate. They start out as an attempt to shield and build into an outward assault. All of these are unconscious protections. Even an attack can be a defensive strategy. Recognizing our defensive tactics can feel confrontive and uncomfortable, but we need to become aware of how they play out in our lives if we are ever to transcend them.

> *"We have lived a childhood of practicing the defensive arts and have become experts in defensive strategies that help us hide the truth."*

The first step in becoming more conscious is to realize what we do that is *not* conscious. Of course, it is easier to see these defensive tendencies in other people, but once we realize that we all have damaged egos, we can begin to accept that we have also adopted automatic defenses.

Let's start by talking about denial. Denial is an easy weapon to recognize. We all do it and also recognize it in others. But denial becomes more intricate when we go a little deeper and look at suppression and repression. Suppression is when something comes up to our awareness and we defensively push it back down. Repression goes deeper yet. It is pushed so far down that we never even know it's there.

Maia used to say, "We all need a little denial, just to get by." There are things that happen in our lives that we need some time to assimilate. Sometimes our vulnerable psyches are not willing to accept things at the moment they occur and impose a protective cushion or shock-absorber of time, if you will. In that moment we either consciously choose to deny to buy ourselves some time to integrate the reality, or our subconscious mind keeps it from our field of awareness until we are ready to see it. This is another example of suppression and repression. It is a spectrum of awareness.

We've been using justifications or reasons in our lives even before our dog ate our homework. These have allowed us to come up with excuses for our behavior and unconscious actions toward ourselves and others. We've wielded them like a defensive weapon to give us an "out" from taking responsibility for ourselves and the things we could have done better. This list is endless, as we all know.

> "We've been using justifications or reasons in our lives even before our dog ate our homework."

Blame is another popular defense. It is so easy to blame others for things that happen in our lives. But as we discussed before, blaming others will render us powerless, and we will find ourselves being at the effect of whatever we blame others for. This is the opposite of being empowered.

Passive/aggressive behavior is so complicated that whole volumes have been written about it. It begins as a coping mechanism adopted by a child to help them get by. I will cover it in more detail in the communication chapter, but as it pertains to defense, I describe it as an attitude of aloofness. Like when we deal with things by retreating into a shell of silence, shutting out others and silencing our own voice. It is the equivalent of wearing noise canceling headphones and a gag over our mouth. No communication comes in and none goes out. Again, there are varying degrees of this, since most of us live in grayscale rather than black and white.

We have all played the victim and used our poor-me attitude so others will feed into the sympathy that "we deserve" because we have been hurt. In reality, sympathy only reinforces the feeling that we are unworthy and undeserving. It feeds the vicious cycle of our victimhood.

Combative is the other end of this spectrum, where we are always fighting to get what "we deserve." But that never gives us a sense of fulfilment. Even if we win the battle, it will always be an empty victory because it comes from our damaged self.

> "...sympathy only reinforces the feeling that we are unworthy and undeserving."

A person who is conflictive is always fighting an inner and outer battle. This is a person who feels attacked much of the time and comes out as the attacker to circumvent these feelings. They are fighting inside themselves because they are not happy or satisfied with how they have shown up in their lives and yet feel the need to defend it. This also comes with an inherent fear that people will see through their facade and judge them harshly. Most of us have known someone like this at some point in our lives. We also have all been this way at one time or another, even if it is not where we reside most of the time.

We have all been criticized and been critical. Some people have learned that in order to feel better about themselves, they need to bring others down. We all learned this behavior as children in a feeble attempt to feel better about ourselves. Unfortunately, it almost certainly backfires, and the shortlived ego satisfaction usually bites us in our proverbial backside.

Our damaged self can't stop judging others as good or bad.

It's just what it does. Our judging self says things like: "I'm not like that," "Yeah, but when I acted like that, I had a good reason, so it's not the same" or "I would never do that."

We need to be aware that this causes a separation from ourselves and whomever we judge harshly. It puts the person who is being judged far apart from the judger in the judger's mind.

When we become aware of our judgments, we can heal this separation by saying to ourselves, "I have been like that," or "I have also acted like that" or "I have done that." In seeing our own imperfections, we are able to forgive others for not being perfect, and we come together rather than cause a rift. It is an awesome practice to correct our thinking and heal the separation. Give it a try. It is simple yet strong.

> "In seeing our own imperfections, we are able to forgive others for not being perfect."

When it comes to defense, attack or intimidation is the "full Monty." If we attack or intimidate others, they will be too apprehensive to inquire as to "who are you in there?" It is the ultimate way of fending off others and keeping them out of our psyches. It is like a brick wall keeping people out of our house of the Self.

Although defensive strategies are employed to protect us, when they are employed by our damaged ego, it causes us to live in a state of perpetual defensiveness. In this state, everyone is an enemy, and we assume that we are being attacked whether or not we are. This condition helps the damaged ego to maintain the status quo where it feels safe and protected. At the same time, it prevents any true personal growth, because true personal evolution includes honest Self-reflection. As long as we are defensive, we are not able to see behind that brick wall. Defensiveness blocks our own view of the Self. When we start taking the bricks out one by one, the foundation will eventually crumble and the whole wall will collapse, leaving us to confront the inner mess our ego has tried so hard to keep hidden. This aversion to facing what is behind that wall is what keeps the damaged ego as the main player in our lives.

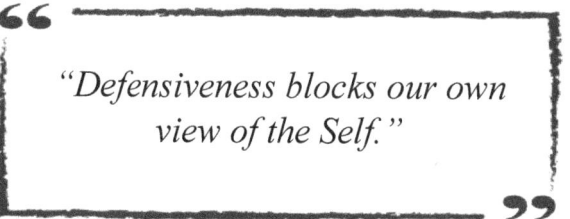

> "Defensiveness blocks our own view of the Self."

We need to remember that even though we cannot be in this physical world without our ego, it is not who we are. We are so much greater than that. We are made from the same dust that forms the stars and planets. We are deeper, wider, and vaster than any of the limitations that have previously defined us. It's time now to start to dis-identify with our egos and to live from the deeper part of ourselves that is limitless.

Can you readily see these defenses in the people around you? It is always easier to notice negative tendencies in others than in ourselves. As a practice, begin observing other people's defensive strategies. It is critical that you do not communicate these observations to anyone. This will be an inner practice. When you become adept at noticing other's defenses, you will be more able to see them in yourself.

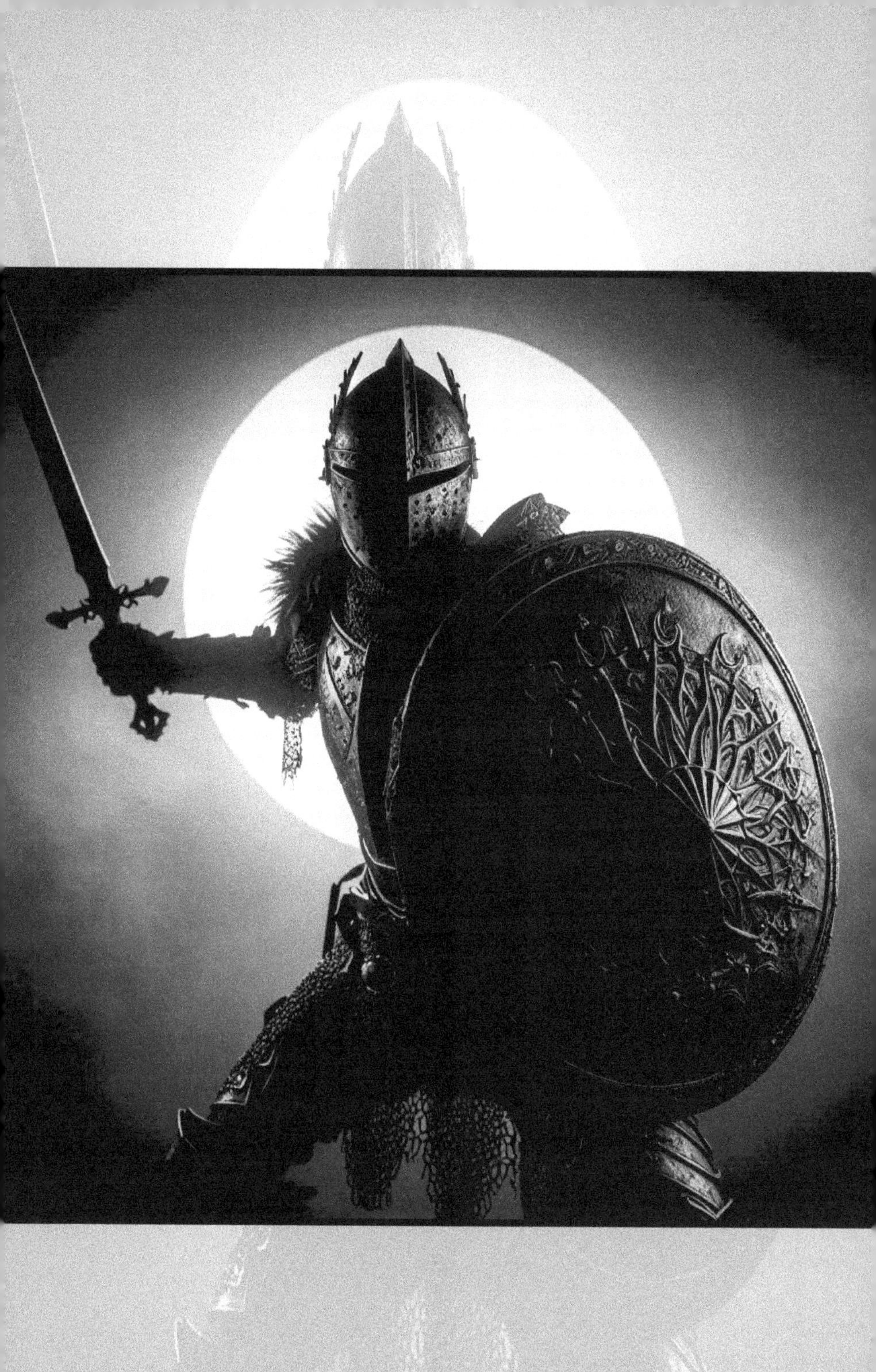

Chapter 6

Communication—A Powerful Gift

True communication is a gift we give others to inform them about what is happening inside of us. Through our words, we are actually taking the perceptions and experiences within us and giving them to another as our truthful and authentic expressions.

Imagine that between you and another there is an invisible space created by your connection. This space can be viewed as a narrow pipe or a wide tunnel, depending on how narrow or broad the connection between you is. If this person represents someone you have little affinity with, that space likely would be narrow or pipe-like. If this person is very important to you in your Life, the space likely would be wider like a tunnel. Either way, this is the line of communication that is used to move information between one another. And until we all have the ability to communicate through our minds, words are the only way to communicate precise thoughts and feelings. Of course, some can perceive body language or sense energy adeptly, but this only gives general feelings, not specifics. We are still dependent on language that can be misinterpreted. This is why we need to be as clear as possible in our communication with others, to minimize the possibility of misinterpretation.

In this chapter we will discuss different aspects of true and non-true communication as well as the withholding of communication. Talking is not necessarily communication, but silence can transmit a thousand words.

True communication, in the context of relationship, happens when we have the courage to risk what we hold close to our hearts, and expose it to others. This makes us vulnerable, and courageous. It requires zero courage to hide, but to expose our inner thoughts, feelings and emotions requires bravery. True communication is the gift we give to others, but also to ourselves. When we openly share from our heart and our sharing is received, we feel connected, heard, cared for and loved.

There are times when others cannot hear us because their emotional triggers are engaged. This is when we must remain as open and courageous as we can. We need to realize that we may not always be accepted or received well, but should not allow our sense of self or self-worth be determined by these outcomes. This is the perfect moment to listen and hear what is said and not close down into our reactivity. By openly listening we may understand why our gift was not accepted. Only by continuing to communicate is there a *possibility* of understanding.

> *"Only by continuing to communicate is there a possibility of understanding "*

You have both come together to create this relationship. Remembering this will help construct the foundation on which these teachings will stand. It is critical to keep our tunnels as wide and clean as possible and do periodic clearing of the space.

Just because someone talks a lot it doesn't mean they are communicating. Endless chatter, gossip and opinions are not true communication. Social interactions have purpose. They are a necessary step as an initial exchange that may lead to a deeper connection. But, at some point we need to choose where we would like to spend the majority of our attention and energy. Do we want to remain in the shallow pools of social interactions, where the bottom is always accessible to our feet? Or swim in the deep waters of meaningful interactions, where we are supported only by the buoyancy of our true Selves?

Only *we* can choose who and how we want to be in our lives. Just keep in mind that when we decide to share ourselves with our partner, it is easier to be swimming at the same end of the pool. If not, there will be quite a bit of yelling, if only to be heard.

Let's assume you are both good communicators and can move freely between shallow and deep communication. This is ideal to keep these teachings alive and vibrant since they require the willingness to dive into the deep.

Earlier I mentioned passive/aggressive behavior is a coping mechanism adopted as children just to get by. If we resort to passive/aggressive behavior often, it was probably a successful tactic *when we were young*. (Passive/aggressive means we are being aggressive even though we appear passive.) This may show up as *not* doing something. Maybe not answering when asked a question or not answering phone calls or texts. You could speak with this person for an hour, and they will sit speechless after everything you have said. But don't get them wrong. They probably really want to respond and participate in the conversation, but as a result of being entrenched in this learned behavior for much of their lives, their mind remains a blank. This type of person has become accustomed to being selfish with their communication. The defense mechanism that worked when they were young is now a habit. One that is difficult to break. The only way for a passive/aggressive to break this habit, if that is what they truly desire, is to continue to communicate. *Say anything*. Even if it feels like the words fall short. This will eventually lead them to the ability to say things at a deeper level. (A valid response would be, "I really want to respond, but I don't know what to say.") This, at least, gives the other person information and a way to continue the dialogue.

> "...passive/aggressive behavior is a coping mechanism adopted as children..."

Being passive/aggressive contributes nothing to the interaction and creates a problem for the communicator who is left with no information to work with. When they ask, "Are you OK?" and the automatic response is, "I'm fine", "I'm fine" represents a brick wall of protection that leaves the communicator, and their questions, out in the cold.

> "Being passive/aggressive contributes nothing to the interaction and creates a problem for the communicator who is left with no information to work with."

If we really want to *create* a relationship, we need to give to the relationship. By giving the powerful gift of communication. A relationship consists of three lives: yours, the other persons, and the relationship itself. If we don't feed the relationship with communication, it could easily wither and die.

True communication will not necessarily keep a relationship alive; Sometimes it runs its course and completes. There may come a time when the reasons that we came together with the other have completed and the lessons need to be integrated in a different space away from one another or simply in a different context. This is when authentic communication helps complete the relationship in a way that causes the least amount of pain. Not by lashing out or avoiding the truth, but by being as truthful as possible, without blame. Where each has an opportunity to grow and evolve.

Are there any aspects of communication that you feel you need work on? Perhaps you feel the need to be more assertive with your communication instead of allowing others to take the reins. Maybe you are a very active talker and need to practice your listening skills more often. Is it possible that you fall in the category of passive/aggressive? If you notice this tendency in others this could be the first step to overcoming its non-generous nature in yourself. Communication is an exchange that flows both ways, with transmitters and receivers on each end. What you say and ask is a contribution to the interaction. You also contribute by listening and receiving.

> *"Communication is an exchange that flows both ways, with transmitters and receivers on each end."*

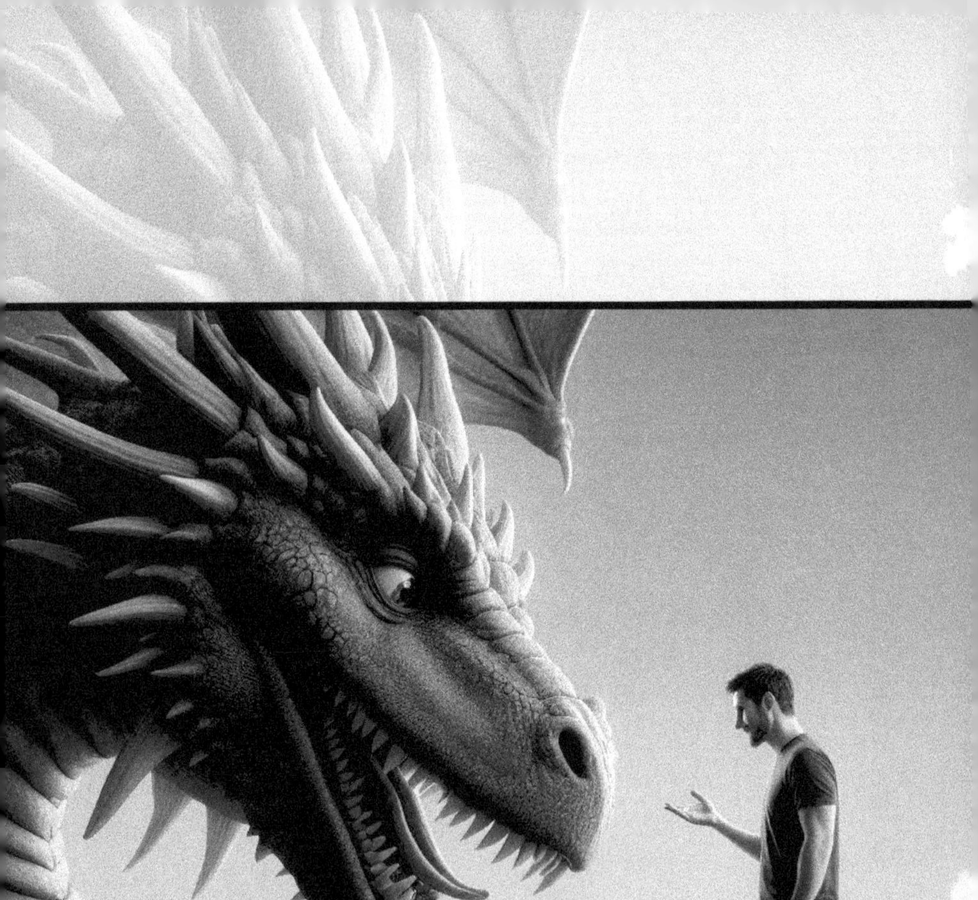

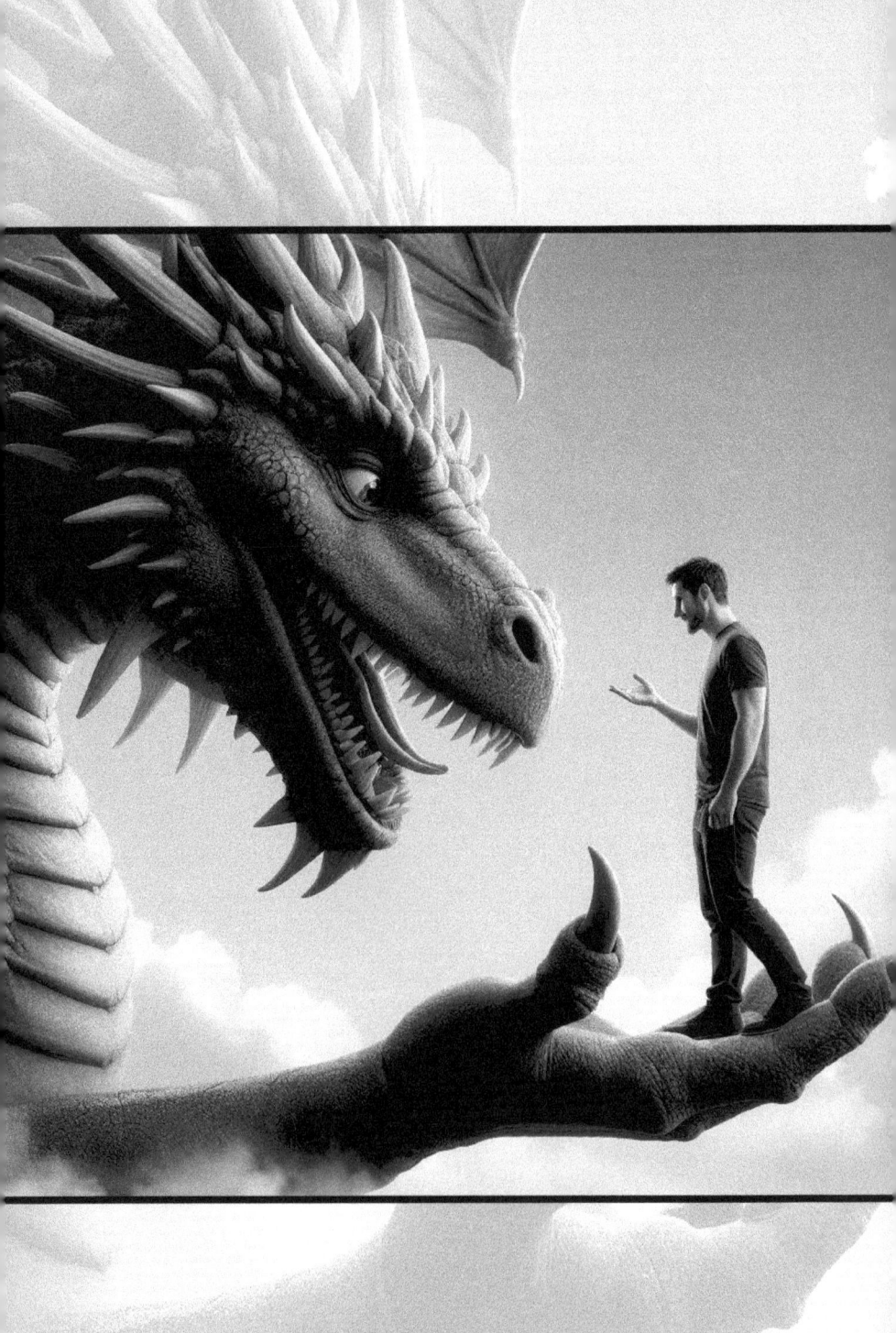

Chapter 7

Keeping Secrets and Lies, Oh My

Secrets and its first cousin, lies, are incredibly detrimental to relationships. They interrupt the natural flow of communication.

Can you keep a secret? If the secret is your own, it may cause you deep shame. Or, if revealed, would put you at risk of an undesirable situation. But secrets get in the way of our true Self.

This happens in various ways. Secrets cause us to feel self-conscious when we communicate. Our attention is on ourselves, to make sure we do not act or say anything that might reveal what we are hiding. We feel uncomfortable if we suspect that someone might know our secret. If we do tell someone, it gives them power over us. They may or may not exercise that power, but we know that if they ever do divulge our secret, we would be at risk. This situation might cause us to act in inauthentic ways toward the secret holder. If we have a disagreement with them, we may not express what we truly feel to avoid the possibility they will reveal our secret.

> "Secrets cause us to feel self-conscious when we communicate."

This is an awful, anxiety-ridden existence. None of us are perfect. We have all done things we are not proud of that cause us deep shame. Instead, imagine feeling free and unconcerned with others' judgements. Our worry about what others might think of us is a trap. The reason we feel shame is because of our *own* judgments about ourselves. We need to do our best to live without secrets and forgive ourselves for what we are ashamed of. They are in the past. We cannot change what has already happened.

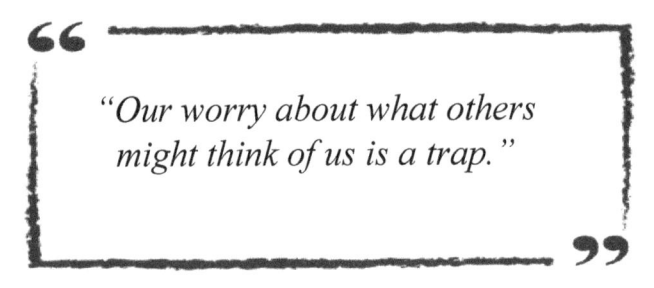

> *"Our worry about what others might think of us is a trap."*

There is always a more conscious way of doing and being. We all have a particular capacity for being conscious at any given moment. Most of us on the journey to become more conscious are doing our best. Even before we began, we were doing our best, given the conditioning, mistreatment, and/or abuse that makes up our past. If we forgive ourselves for our past; for our regrets; we would release the emotional energies tied up in them and lay them to rest. In a world where trust is often betrayed, if we are fortunate enough to find someone we feel safe with to share our burdens and know our trust will be upheld, it would be a blessing. What a weight off our psyches!

The following is a true story of another kind of secret that can be quite detrimental.

Peter lives with his Uncle Jarod and Aunt Jenna, who are living in the house his mother, Sharon, owns while she is abroad for a few years. On one of Sharon's visits back home, she says to Peter, "I have to tell you something that Jenna said about you, but you cannot tell her what I told you." She proceeds to tell him some negative comments Jenna shared with her. At this point Peter becomes upset with Jenna, but he agreed not to say anything to her and feels obligated to sit on it.

This happens more often than one can imagine. What actually happened is Sharon wanted to gossip but didn't want it traced back to her. So, she pulled a promise out of Peter in exchange for satisfying his natural curiosity about the information offered. Sharon had little consideration to how this could affect the relational tension of the household. Peter would hold covert resentment toward Jenna, which would undoubtedly be displayed with signs of hostility and create an unpleasant environment. Basically, Sharon caused Peter an emotional upset with Jenna then tied his hands, or in this case, his tongue. This agreement bound him to silence. With no way to express his resentment or anger, depending on the harshness of the comments from Jenna. Without an opportunity to clear the space between them no resolution could occur.

I have found an easy solution to this. If someone says, "I need to tell you something about someone," I ask, "Will what you plan to say cause me an emotional upset with them? If so, I will clear it with them directly. I will not keep this kind of secret. So, think about what it is you *need* to tell me." After this clarification, the person usually does not share the gossip.

Another thing that disrupts the flow of communication is *lies*. This is a touchy subject. Nobody likes being lied to. It causes a sense of betrayal that cuts deep. The interesting thing is, even people who lie often, hate being lied to. How ironic.

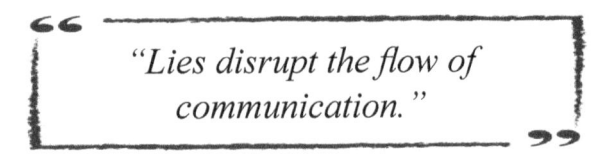

> "Lies disrupt the flow of communication."

There are different severities to lies; no two lies are created equal. However, all lies block our ability to naturally communicate. Remember our pipe or tunnel through which communication travels? A lie is like a boulder in our tunnel. The bigger the lie, the bigger the boulder. If the lie is small and insignificant, our communication can find a way around it to reach the recipient. But, if the lie is huge and important, our communication has no way around it. The silence and discomfort caused is undeniable.

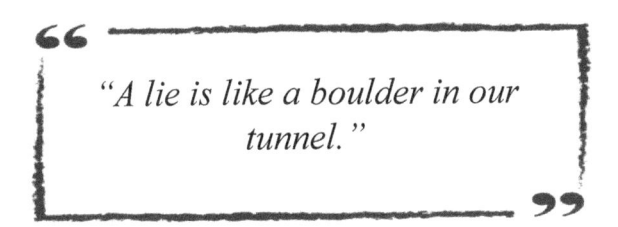

> "A lie is like a boulder in our tunnel."

We are talking about true communication, which is the opposite of a lie. Hence the dilemma. When we are in true relationship, and we lie to cover up a misdeed or mistake (often because we are apprehensive about the other's reaction), we feel uncomfortable in their presence, which causes a separation. Communication becomes crippled. We may be able to talk superficially, but our discomfort is so present that it feels unnatural and forced, and we feel self-conscious.

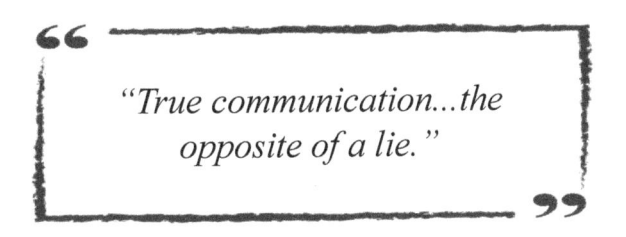

> "True communication...the opposite of a lie."

Go back to when you lied to someone you loved. How did it feel to be dishonest with them? How did it change your relationship? Did it cause your Love to diminish? Think about how you may have justified the lie by convincing yourself that you did it to save them pain. That the truth would hurt them. It may be true, but a lie is always more painful than the truth. Because no matter how painful, the truth gives the person the necessary information to make an intelligent choice.

> *"...a lie is always more painful than the truth."*

We are intelligent beings. Most can feel when they are being lied to. There are glaring signals. When the liar thinks we suspect their deception, their emotional reaction is disproportionate to the situation. The person lying might fly into a rage; including blame or accusations that leave the recipient baffled and confused. We do not know *what* is happening, but we know *something* is happening. Most likely a lie is clogging the pipe of communication, or a big boulder is lodged in the tunnel and blocking the space of love.

There are some so used to lying that they are accustomed to this unease. In fact, it has become their comfort zone. They probably would not read this book! But if you are, then you likely want to live your life more in truth than lies.

No wonder, "The truth will set you free," is still used often today. Keeping secrets and lies is a life sentence where truth is the only key to unlock the cell.

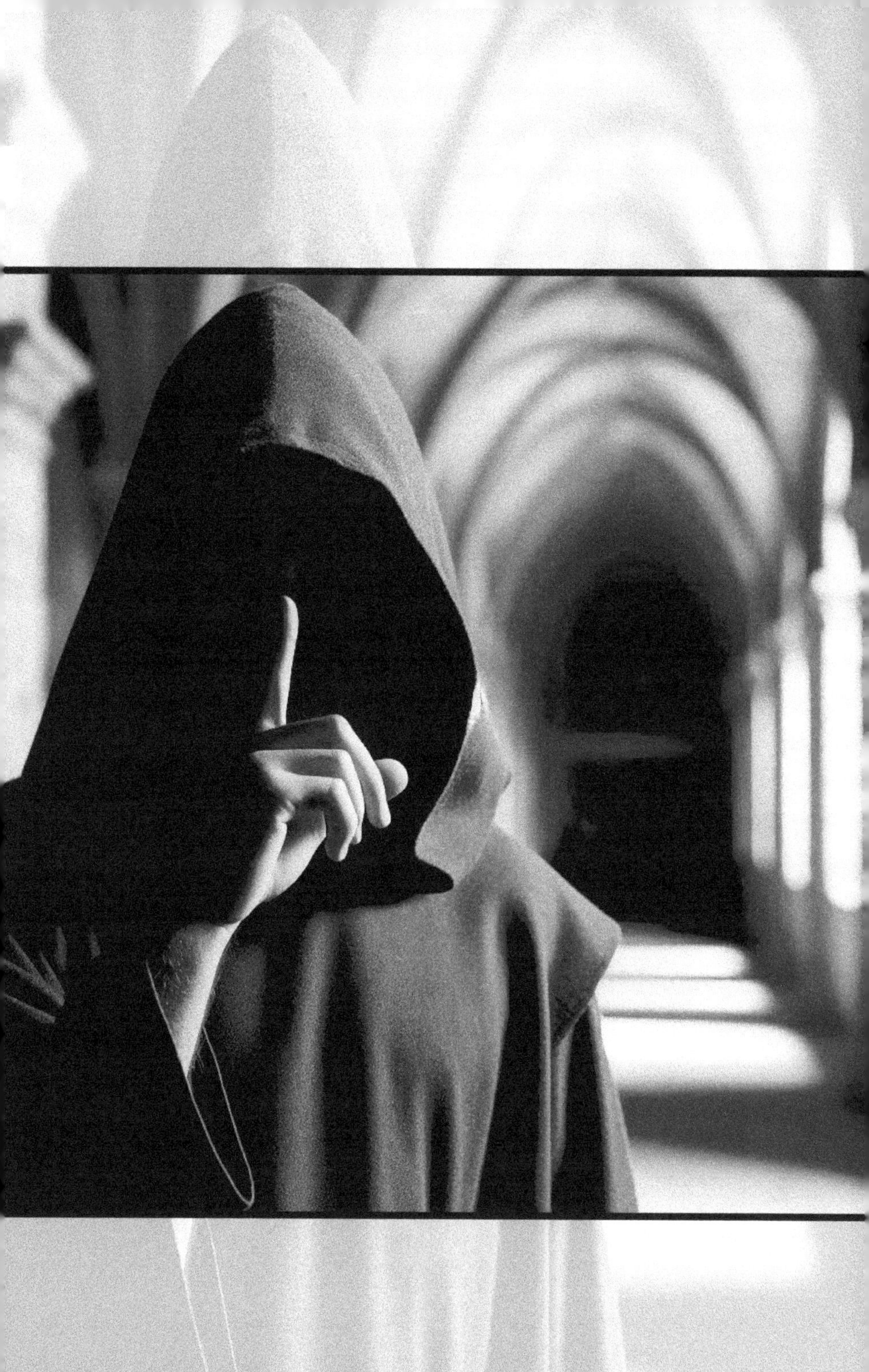

Chapter 8

You Hold My Space and I'll Hold Yours

When we join together with another person to create a relationship, we bring into being a new life form—the relationship itself. It is brought into existence by the co-mingling of energies that each person contributes, along with the intention to bring it into being.

Once born, the relationship follows a path all its own. To sustain the relationship, it needs energy, attention, and intention, although it can complete even when we nourish it. Once the honeymoon stage is over, we need to continuously remind each other that we are on the same team. This requires awareness that our pasts will be triggered by each other. It is easy to confuse the finger that pulled the trigger in the present with the actual enemy: our past unconscious pain and wounds. In order to heal our pasts, we need to hold each other's space.

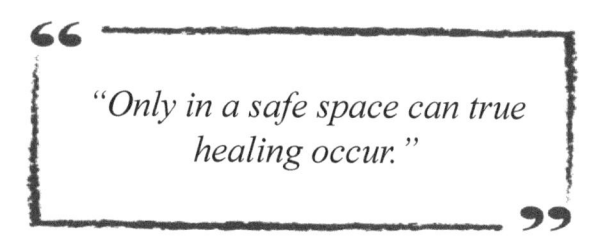

> *"Only in a safe space can true healing occur."*

Let's define this space. A *safe* space, free of judgments, expectations and demands. Only in a safe space can true healing occur.

Take a moment to become aware of where you feel most safe. Somewhere you feel totally free to be who you are, without expectations, judgments or demands. It is vital we have this space so we can rest from the constant pressure of the complex world we live in and reset. Why do you think so many people suffer from diseases whose origin is stress? Many people do not have a safe place to reset.

Take a moment to identify if there is a person who represents a safe space for you. A person you can fully be yourself with. The good, the bad; the beautiful, and ugly; the loving, the fearful. Someone who allows you to just be. To act, react, express, or be silent, to be angry or sad. If you have even one person who can be that, you are truly blessed. They hold a space in their being in which you feel safe and loved no matter what.

> *"It is vital we have this space so we can rest from the constant pressure of the complex world we live in and reset."*

When we are in a relationship, we must be able to provide a safe space for each other. We do this by reminding ourselves that we are only the finger that pulled the trigger and activated someone's past pain. It may erupt right in front of us, but it is really not about us. We need to be free from that eruption and be a witness to the pain that spews out.

> *"...we are only the finger that pulled the trigger and activated someone's past pain."*
> *It's not about us. We need to depersonalize it.*

In any relationship, both partners need to take turns holding the space for the other. We need to be greater than our reactivity and hurt, when it's our turn. Even when our drama wants to trump their drama, we need to hold it in check and allow them to have their say. We do our best to remember that they are filtering the present through their past experiences. This creates a particular reality, and it is one hundred percent valid to them.

Once done, we can share our perceptions and experiences, and even our drama. That's when it's their turn to hold the space for us. After all, what makes one person's perception truer than another's? Have you heard it said that we create our own reality? This is priceless to keep in mind when facing another's viewpoint that is different from your own.

I've recently realized one particular attitude that renders us incapable of holding the space for another: victimhood. The person who plays the perpetual victim is forever searching to twist what we say into attacks or criticisms.

When you say, "Your place is nice, I didn't picture it like this," they respond with, "What, did you think I lived in a dump?"

You say, "You look nice today." They respond, "Didn't I look nice yesterday?"

You get the picture.

Victimhood is a coping mechanism adopted at a young age to elicit sympathy and fend off attacks and negative attention. The child adopting this persona lessons the possibility or severity of the attacks and negative attention. Once again, the coping mechanisms that worked so well as children become difficult to overcome as adults. The victim will automatically view and portray themselves as *the* injured party to gain the "importance" their wounds represent, thereby gaining attention. Many times, these wounds are used as leverage to manipulate others into doing or acting in a particular way. Since the victim is all about themselves and **their suffering**. In this state of victimhood, it is impossible for them to hold the space for anyone else. If someone else expresses pain their pain is *always* worse. If someone else cries they rapidly cry along. If someone else is angry that person is being mean. If someone needs time alone, they feel rejected. It is difficult to share thoughts and feelings with someone who takes *everything personally*. It feels like walking through a mine field when we are interacting with a victim. We never know what will cause an explosion of "poor me".

> *Holding space for another requires focused concern for another's well-being.*
> *Victimhood's only concern is self.*

To hold the space for another, we need to drop our judgments, expectations and demands and allow space for their humanity. No matter what. Many times, a silent safe space—containing no advice, solutions, or opinions—is the way we may best serve others.

Now we have a better understanding of what it means to hold space for one another:

Do you remember when you did not hold that space for someone, and a disagreement erupted and led to further upset? In hindsight, you might recognize what determined your inability to hold space for them. Was it judgment of how they behaved or *the way* they said what they said? Was it a defense you employed that closed off their ability to express their perceptions and feelings?

On the other side, do you remember when you tried to communicate with someone who did not allow you to fully express yourself? Was there any defense on their part? How did you feel?

It is important to experience both sides. To become aware of how we are affected, and how we affect others.

You hold my space and I'll hold yours.

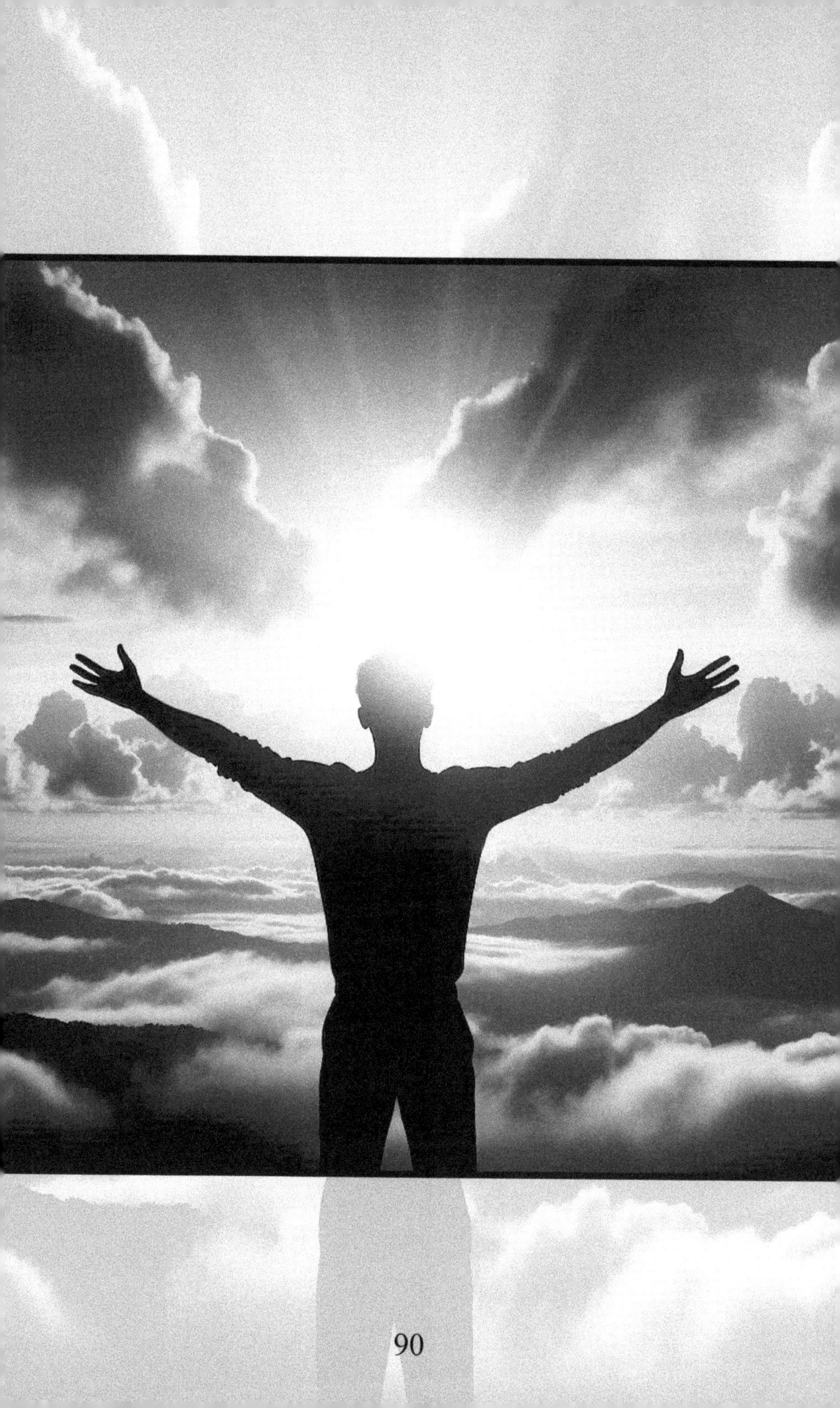

Chapter 9

Our Minds Doing Algebra – Solving The X-Factor

Our analytical mind is the problem-solving component of our being. It does the best job with the information presented. Calculating all the possibilities of the future, with the information presented in the now; combined with the pertinent information from the past, our mind tries to formulate a logical solution of possible future outcomes. Even explaining this in a mindful (pardon the pun) manner is like attempting to untangle a massive ball of twine. There are so many variables that it's mind-boggling.

Of course, we can guess at the most likely possibility, but as the universe is so infinite, with infinite elements of the unknown, that it's impossible to calculate. Still, our minds won't stop doing what they were created to do: solve the problem at hand. Whether that is devising a new, more efficient, way to complete our tasks; or behaving in the best way to have our needs met with our relationships. The problem, in all situations, is the X-factor: *the unknown*. In algebra, the formulas are created to determine X. If X equals this, then *this* is the answer; if X equals that, then *that* is the answer.

In personal relationships, X equals the human element. This is the mystery that each person contains in their being. We can never really know how our partner processes their perceptions, or what hidden elements are at play. Given the vast unconsciousness that lives inside us, we cannot be aware of all the elements contained inside our own being! Not to mention, the infinite mysteries of the universe.

One approach to this seemingly unsolvable problem is to imagine one probable outcome but remain open to other possibilities. In other words, do your best not to attach to a particular outcome.

If we are attached to how we would like things to be, we may feel disappointment more often than not. When we attach ourselves to one particular possibility, we are placing our happiness on the winning numbers of our Life's lottery. If other numbers are drawn, we won't feel happy, and we will experience disappointment. Becoming attached to the way things "should be" invariably causes us to act or respond inauthentically. Because we don't want to risk our desired outcome, we may edit our true feelings and say only what will help create our desire.

My spiritual teacher often said, *"You are not responsible for any outcome; you are only responsible to be the truth of yourself in every moment of your Life and let the chips fall where they may."* The commitment to being the truth of ourselves has to outweigh the fear of losing our attachments, of not having things go exactly as we want and knowing we cannot control the future. Thinking *we can* manipulate others to act in ways we desire, in order to create future outcomes, is what leads us to inauthentic behavior. When we make the commitment to ourselves that, no matter what the risks, we will be as truthful and authentic as we are capable of in the moment, that choice will live inside us and will be the determining factor of our Self-expression. This is the *Hero's Journey.*

We also need to be conscious of our highest good in each moment. For example, if someone points a gun at you, the highest choice may not be to express anger or outrage. This may get you shot. So, you keep quiet and know you are not confusing courage with stupidity.

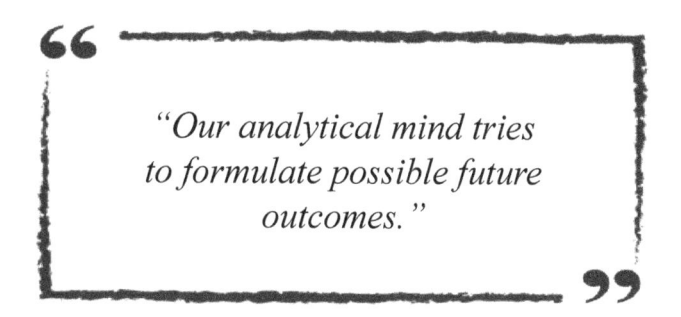

> *"Our analytical mind tries to formulate possible future outcomes."*

Our computing mind does not like blank spaces. Whenever our mind is presented with a blank space, it attempts to fill it. Our minds automatically draw conclusions and assumptions when there is missing information. In fact, it can creatively come up with conclusions and assumptions that may likely be erroneous. For example, if your boyfriend is late, he is probably cheating. When he says he will call at five p.m. but it's six-thirty—he doesn't care because he didn't call. Maybe he's had an accident or is in the hospital and cannot call. If we ask a question and he doesn't answer, he's hiding something. If he is distracted and not paying attention to us, he is affirming we are not worthy of his Love. Given the many disappointments in our past, our minds too often come up with negative conclusions that cause worry, pain, loss or upset.

These unconscious trenches from our past traumas are so easily slipped into. They become insidious traps for our minds. This is when we need to step in with conscious awareness and correct our thinking. We must remind ourselves that we only know what we know. That our boyfriend is late, or he has not called. or we asked him a question and he has not answered— that is *all* we know. The rest is our mind automatically filling in the blanks.

Here is an example. Mario and Steve are in a committed

relationship for a few of years. Steve's birthday is next month, and Mario has decided to throw him a surprise party. Mario is not accustomed to keeping secrets and is a bit unsure how to keep it for a month. But he is so excited about surprising Steve that he is willing to make a valiant effort with his acting ability. While watching TV, Steve notices Mario replying to a text in an uncharacteristic way but thinks nothing of it. Mario would never do anything disloyal, so Steve brushes away the thought.

The next week, Mario steps onto the balcony, and Steve hears him on the phone. When he asks Mario who he was talking to, he says his brother. Steve feels something is off about his response. Now, Steve is beginning to feel unsure and suspicious. Something feels wrong, but he cannot put his finger on it. He knows Mario is uncomfortable about something, but not wanting to cause Mario an upset or create conflict by voicing his doubt, he says nothing. He decides to be super vigilant to see what he might uncover. A dark part of Steve's past becomes triggered, which includes disappointment with others that were not honest with him and were disloyal. This brings up unresolved energies of betrayal, pain and loss—initiating suspicions about Mario that Steve does not even want to think about. Nonetheless, they float up toward his mind as sure as air bubbles rise to the surface.

Lately, Steve notices that Mario is communicating with

many people that neither regularly speak with. Mario seems very uncomfortable when Steve asks questions. Mario's evasiveness is confirming Steve's fear that Mario is lying to him, frequently. Steve can no longer wait and asks Mario, "Is everything OK? Do you still Love me?"

Mario is so hurt by the question that his anger flares. "How can you ask me that!? Of course, I Love you! I show you that every day!"

This reaction only causes more insecurity for Steve, and now he *knows* that Mario is cheating on him. Mario is unusually quiet and distant, which only confirms Steve's suspicions. As time passes, Steve feels unable to tolerate the uncertainty that this truth creates in him. They plan to go out to dinner on Saturday night on Steve's birthday, and Steve plans to break up with Mario then. He cannot tolerate lies, especially to cover up being cheated on again.

They valet the car and enter the restaurant. Mario tells the hostess that they have a reservation under Perez and are escorted to a back room. When they open the door, everything is dark; Steve is unsure what is happening. Suddenly the lights turn on, and a big crowd yell, *"HAPPY BIRTHDAY!"* Steve turns to Mario with tears rolling down his I-can't-believe-this face. Mario wipes his tears, "Happy Birthday, baby … I Love you so much. I thought I'd never be able to keep this surprise from you, but I guess I did a pretty good job. Though, I thought you were catching on a few times. Hahaha!"

Can you imagine how Steve is feeling? He was ready to end a relationship based on his assumptions about what was happening with Mario. He turned his imagined fear into truth, based on his history of being lied to and cheated on. The relief must be staggering, knowing that, what Mario was hiding, was a gesture of Love and celebration, not infidelity and deceit.

We also do the opposite of this. When we meet someone new and imagine a whole future based on our initial feelings of emotional connectedness, while in our honeymoon phase. (Sometimes, this happens after only a few days of texts.) We do not even know how this person will respond in the face of adversity or emotional turmoil. Suddenly, we are confronted with a person who, isn't at all like the person we experienced during the initial phase. We can now see how they respond when the chips are down, and the emotional stuff of their past is ignited. Sometimes they are unwilling to participate in the difficult work to maintain a relationship. If this happens, we not only suffer the loss of this person, but also the intense disappointment of a future we made up in our heads. Just because it wasn't real does not mean we do not suffer its loss.

That loss gets tangled into the other disappointments we've suffered when Life did not turn out the way we wanted or imagined. The loss is intense.

Do the math. We only know what we know and nothing more. While our minds do algebra, remember to leave the X factor in as an unknown, and remain open to all possibilities. Sometimes the outcome is better than we could have imagined.

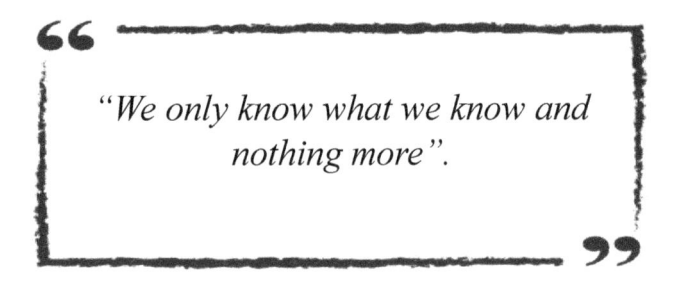

> *"We only know what we know and nothing more".*

Can you remember believing something you made up in your mind that turned out to be untrue? When I was a child, I imagined many fearful possibilities when my parents arrived home later than expected. I felt great relief on their arrival. Do you remember feeling this way as a child?

Can you remember romanticizing a future when you met someone you were attracted to? Perhaps, imagined when you would move in together. That you would be together for a long time, or even "forever." Because of your attraction, you could swear you felt their attraction just as strongly. When the fantasy ended, did it feel disproportionate to the length of time you knew one another? Maybe other aspects were somehow augmented by the mental romance? It is very difficult to reel in our mind when it fabricates these imaginative scenarios.

In those cases, we might talk to ourselves and say, "Stop making things up! You only know that your parents are late." or "You don't know where this relationship is going. Let it evolve as it should."

101

Chapter 10

Can You Get to Gratitude?

In the summer of 1992, I assisted my teacher Maia with a spiritual retreat at a property off a winding road leading to the Santa Fe ski valley. We were three miles up the foothills in a majestic terrain of trails, wrapped in aromatic pines full of pine nuts and crunchy needles under our feet. The dry heat seemed to intensify the scent of nature and uplift the spirit.

On the third day of the retreat Maia assessed the participants by asking how they were. When it was Dina's turn to share, she started to complain that her back hurt and how she had not slept well because of the discomfort of her bed. She went on to her dislike of oatmeal, which was our usual breakfast served with chopped nuts, fruit, and vanilla yogurt. She was obviously in a negative state of mind because of her particular preferences and restless night's sleep.

Maia said something to the effect of, "Dina, is there any way that you can get to gratitude?" Dina was resistant and said she did not know. Maia continued, "We are in Santa Fe, New Mexico; in the beautiful foothills of the ski valley; on this amazing property; surrounded by nature and like-minded individuals. Your spiritual process is being served by teachings, processes, dancing, singing, and meditation; and your mind is stuck on your bed and preferences of breakfast. Can you come up with one thing that you are grateful for right now?" Dina was incapable of finding something to be grateful for. This frame of mind dominated her state of being for the rest of that day before she was able to come around.

> *"There is always something to be grateful for!"*

This is just one way that your mind blocks your ability to experience gratitude. When you become fixated on your preferences and your particular set of parameters of how you want things to be, you do not allow yourselves to see what is right in front of you. There is always something to be grateful for!

I've also noticed a human tendency to take for granted people, situations, talents, or blessings that are at our fingertips and consistently within our reach. For example, when was the last time you were truly grateful for a breath? When last were you in awe of the innate ability to take air into your lungs? Imagine that someone with super strength has your head submerged under water at the deep end of a pool; holding your head down for only a minute—but time is crawling in slow motion—and a minute seems like an hour. Imagine how in the last few seconds of submersion you struggle to not gag-in for breath, which would only flood your lungs with chlorinated water. Now bring yourself to the moment when you are allowed to come up and take a full, deep breath. Can you imagine how grateful you will be when you take that fresh air into your burning lungs?

> *Feel the blessing of breathing freely by taking a slow deep breath and releasing it.*

Most of us are blessed with the ability to breathe freely, and it happens unconsciously. We give it no thought because it is always available to us. How many things in your Life do you take for granted in this way? Take a moment to reflect on some of the things you could find gratitude for in your Life, but because of their constant presence, you do not quite appreciate.

Another way to find gratitude is to acknowledge that everything is perfect in your life. Thanks to your experiences and journey, you are where you are, which is perfect and will lead you to the next necessary phase. You come to realize that in your narrow scope of your life's process, you made judgments about certain occurrences that have blocked your gratitude toward your life's path.

Try to recall a time when you experienced a difficult or challenging situation; maybe a breakup, the loss of a job, or other circumstances where you suffered loss. How many times during that difficulty did you wish you weren't going through it? *If only this or that would not have led to the beginning of the end*, you think. And then time passed and brought you to a new season, with a new relationship, a new job, or a new circumstance, and you realized that you were so joyful to be brought to this place. Perhaps you even thought about that difficult situation and how: even though it was not easy and included pain and suffering: it was a necessary step to your new reality. That struggle enabled you to find your way to a new place of happiness.

In truth, no matter what difficulty we've experienced in Life, however painful, there is always value to be deciphered from it. When we are in the thick of it, we will not be able to perceive the lessons or growth that will emerge after the crisis has passed, maybe not for some time. And, of course, none of us can see the light when we are lost in the midst of a dark time. More than likely, we will not be able to connect to any feelings of gratitude. This is the perfect time to remind ourselves that everything is temporary; this too shall pass. We may not be able to see the perfection, but somehow it *is* perfect.

At some point in our unfoldment, as we become more conscious, we will stop making the pain and struggle of our past wrong and realize that it was a necessary element to bring us to where we are. It is all part of the journey. This will allow us to naturally feel our gratitude. Had we known beforehand what we would have to endure, we never would have travelled that path. However, having done so has made us stronger, more resilient, and expanded within ourselves.

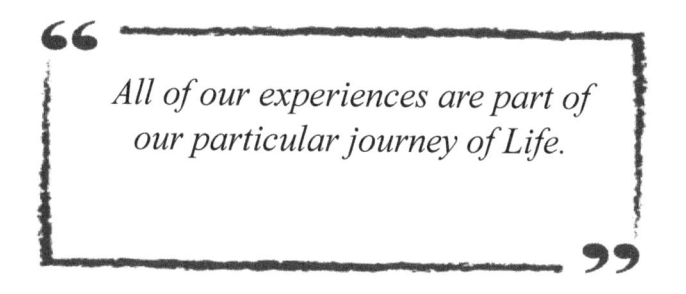

> *All of our experiences are part of our particular journey of Life.*

Let's discuss gratitude in the context of a relationship. In my view, if you approach a relationship out of need, you will most likely be left wanting. Many of us go into a relationship because we feel a void within ourselves, and we try to fill that void through someone else. This emptiness comes from feelings of disconnectedness, unworthiness, and lack of Self-Love which can only be filled from within. Nothing and no one else is capable of filling your inner emptiness. While it seems as though this other person has the ability to make you happy, this fantasy can last only so long. Not to mention that putting that responsibility on someone else is a huge burden. Eventually other people will lose their ability to fulfill this quest—to satisfy your desire to be happy—because only *you* can choose to be happy. If you begin a relationship with a need to complete yourself through another, you will soon feel dissatisfied and start to view the glass-of-relationship as half empty.

If you want to be in a relationship because you are unhappy alone, you are bringing your *unhappy-aloneness* to the relationship. This causes problems in several ways. One, the probability is high that you are likely to settle for someone who is not a good match for you, rather than facing being alone. Two, whatever your partner can bring will fall short in your perception; and three, this situation makes it difficult to truly feel gratitude.

If you are fulfilled in your aloneness, if you feel connected, worthy of love and you love yourselves, then you bring that fullness to share with the other. In this reality, since you are not in a state of need, whatever your partner is willing or capable of sharing with you will be appreciated and valued.

We live in a world full of miracles and are privileged to be present during a time of tremendous change and evolution. As a result, there are many realities and viewpoints existing simultaneously, which can be confusing. We are constantly being pulled in every direction, and our attention is being drawn into thoughts that can polarize us and cause us to feel conflict. Do your best not to get absorbed into the negativity that surrounds you. We all have more than enough reasons to fight with one another, let's find reasons to connect and honor each other. We are at choice as to where to focus our attention; choose to focus on the positive—inside and out. Find things in your Life that you can be grateful for. Let's get to gratitude.

> *"...if you feel connected, worthy of love and you love yourselves, then you bring that fullness to share with the other."*

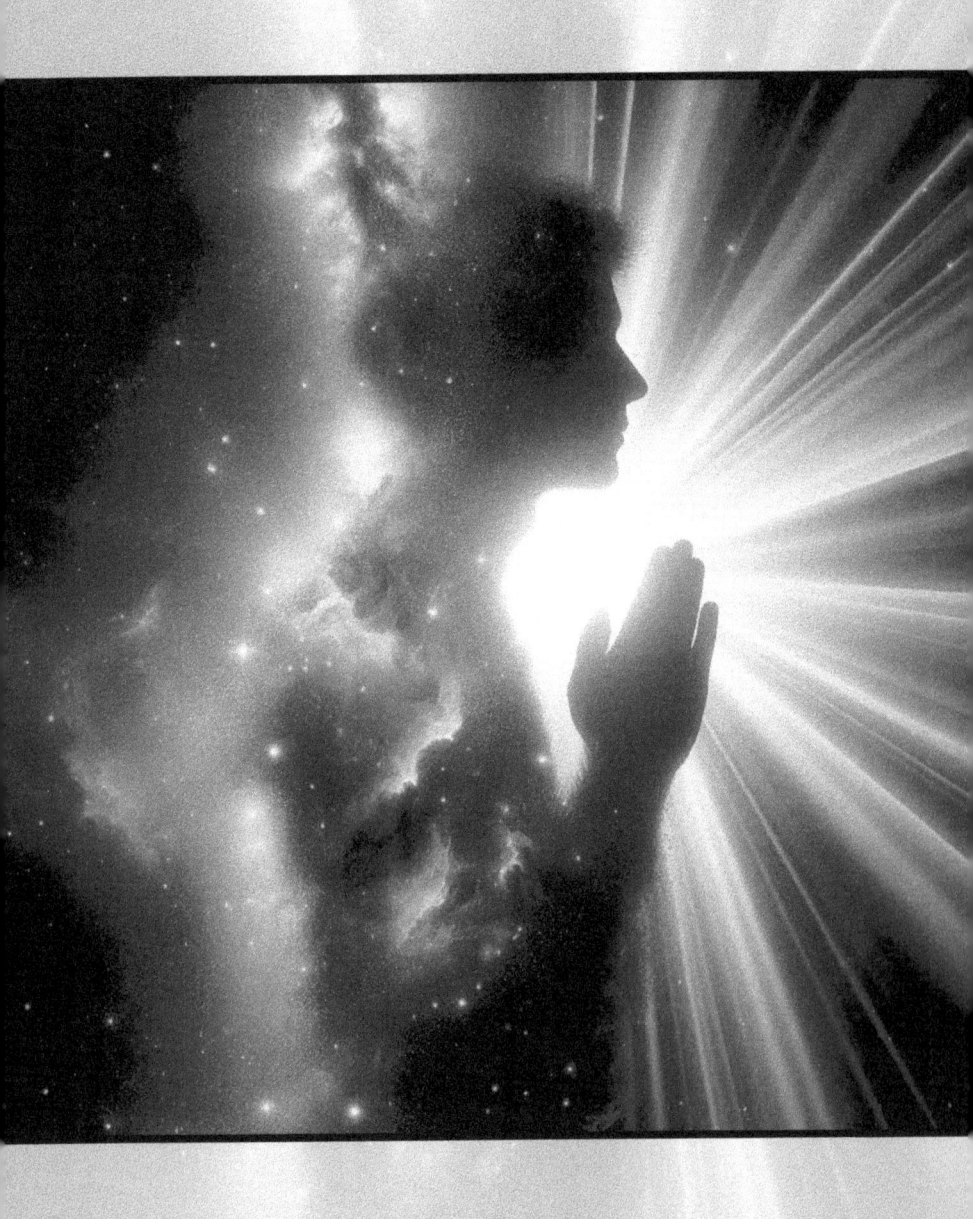

Chapter 11

I'll Never Do That Again—Life's Lessons

Frequently I have heard people say, "I'll never do *that* again." I have observed that they often respond this way after a painful experience, as if they can actually avoid Life's upsetting circumstances by not putting themselves at risk or not acting in ways that will attract pain. From my own observation, living a pain-free Life in this tumultuous world is less than probable. I would say the odds are better at winning the Powerball. We have been taught as children that pain is bad, and pleasure is good. And most of us spend a great deal of energy trying to avoid pain, conflict, and difficulty. We do this by taking the easy way out. We avoid saying how we feel because we lack the courage to be honest and open about our feelings. This behavior backfires on us more often than we care to admit. It also leaves us feeling conflicted within ourselves, because we are not being loyal to our true Self-expression.

Is a painful experience truly a bad thing if it has the potential to propel us into our own evolution? Think back in your Life and remember the times when you have experienced the most personal growth. Would you say those times of greatest growth are usually after experiences of crisis or pain? Most would agree this is the case.

The truth is—the ego will not change unless it has to. If the ego feels as though it is able to get by in a *comfort zone* that is not very fulfilling, but not so awful either, its fear of change will be dominant and likely prevail. The pain caused by unconsciousness in our lives will need to outweigh the fear of the ego to change in order for growth to occur. When that happens, the ego will let go of control long enough to let the greater Self drive for a period of time, hopefully long enough to put some meaningful mileage on our Life's odometer.

> *"For those of us who have made the courageous choice to be authentic, with all that it entails, we are constantly being tested in that choice."*

For those of us who have made the courageous choice to be authentic, with all that it entails, we are constantly being tested in that choice. When we start a new relationship and begin to express to the other person who we are, we naturally put our best self forward. Nobody wants to begin a relationship with their imperfections and shortcomings, so we generally tuck those things out of view. Keep in mind too, that the other person is most likely doing the same. In the beginning of a relationship there is probably little cause for our egos to be triggered.

As time passes, and more familiarity is acquired, we may gain insights into the other person that offer us the opportunity to see aspects of their personality or qualities we have not been privy to before. When the time comes to express feelings or thoughts, we feel may not be accepted or agreed with, the real testing begins. This is when our commitment to being the truth of ourselves needs to outweigh the fear of possible rejection or disagreement. We will always need to make the higher choice that supports our truth, and each time we do, it will become a bit easier.

Remember, everything is a *practice* in Life. That is why successful people do not consider setbacks a failure; they are practicing success. No one expects to take up skiing or skating; for example, without ever losing their balance. They are learning, which includes falling on their backside and hitting the snow or pavement occasionally. No one would fault them for falling, so why are we so hard on ourselves when we fall short of our expectations? That's when we need to forgive ourselves, pick ourselves up, correct the damage and try to do better.

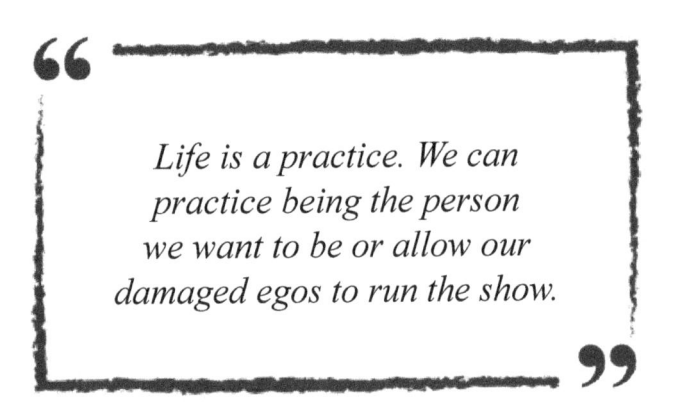

> *Life is a practice. We can practice being the person we want to be or allow our damaged egos to run the show.*

Now that we have Life's practice in perspective, what about compassion for others and their practice as well? This includes forgiving others for their mistakes and imperfect attempts at practicing being a better human.

When I was twenty, I met my first live-in boyfriend, Jordy. We were swept up in our attraction for each other and had a good level of communication, but we never really spoke of commitment or exclusivity. After three months, I learned that he had been with someone else. He said that he was trying to prove to himself that he was not falling in Love with me, but he failed in his attempt and felt awful about it. I told him that I had no right to be angry with him because we never spoke about exclusivity. However, from that moment on, I was not willing to continue our relationship without a commitment. At first, he was very resistant, but I was not willing to bend on this point; he finally agreed to be exclusive.

Of course, this did not inspire much confidence for me and after a couple of months I got to a breaking point. I told him if he could not help me feel more at ease about trusting him, I would not last much longer in this relationship. (I tended to take drastic measures to obtain a feeling of security. If we weren't together, I wouldn't have to worry.) At work I often found myself thinking about all the things that he might be doing with other guys. After a long conversation, and feeling his sincerity, I accepted his assurances that being with other guys was the furthest thing from his mind; that helped put me at ease. After that, he would occasionally bring up the possibility of having an open relationship so that if any slip-up did occur, we would not have to split up because of it. We both had good communication skills and, somehow, I understood he was trying to anticipate things that might happen in the distant future and protect the relationship.

A few months later—at age twenty-one and eager for experience—I felt I might want to experiment and take advantage of an open relationship. So, the next time he brought it up, I agreed to it. In the following months I had a couple of experiences which I communicated to Jordy. Then

I met Freddy, my second live-in boyfriend.

I was convinced I would find my true happiness with Freddy. But in the process of ending my relationship with Jordy, I caused him tremendous pain, something I really didn't want to do. We'd had a very good experience together, even though the intensity of my feelings for him had waned after a while. I could not, however, be deterred from trying to find my happiness with Freddy. I know within myself, that if there were any way I could have been happy with Freddy without causing Jordy so much pain, I would surely have chosen that. Unfortunately, his pain was inevitable, and it caused me great guilt. The end of the relationship with Jordy was a hard lesson that is still providing me with wisdom some forty years later.

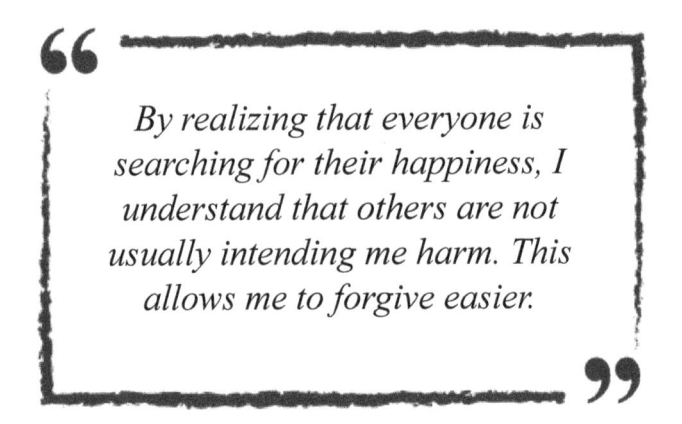

> *By realizing that everyone is searching for their happiness, I understand that others are not usually intending me harm. This allows me to forgive easier.*

Ever since that experience, I look at people in the following way: most people are intrinsically good, and they are just looking for their own happiness. When people act in ways that cause me pain, I know they are probably not intending to hurt me. They are just doing what they feel they need to do to find their happiness and are not considering the effects of their actions on me. Or maybe they are just doing a poor job at making wise choices which lessens the possibility of negative consequences. Even people who do (seemingly) bad things are probably thinking; in some twisted psyche kind of way; that those things will somehow bring them happiness. Like the person who feels they need to put others down to feel good about themselves, or who criticizes others to be self-righteous. By looking at people in this way, I am able to forgive them faster and move on, allowing them their process of becoming a better human being while I practice becoming one as well.

How we choose to deal with pain, crisis and difficulty in life is on a spectrum. At one end of the spectrum, we try to avoid pain at all costs; at the other end, we dwell, wallow, and relive it. I feel it's best to find a balance. We need to allow ourselves to experience the pain when it swells up in us, express and expel the emotional energies associated with it, then move on to be fully available for the next experience Life will gift us with.

If you ever hear yourself saying, "I'll never do *that* again," try to remember that Life's lessons are never about contraction, of becoming less or smaller. Life's lessons will always be about expansion and becoming greater than we were before. Keep putting yourself out there; risk getting hurt and trampled on—try not to search for ways to feel hurt or betrayed—but if you find you are experiencing pain, allow it. Realize it is your own reality; try to decipher what the pain is saying to you and allow it to be expressed. If we protect ourselves from pain, we cut ourselves off from Life and Love. We cannot fear and Love simultaneously; we can occupy only one side of the continuum at a time, not both.

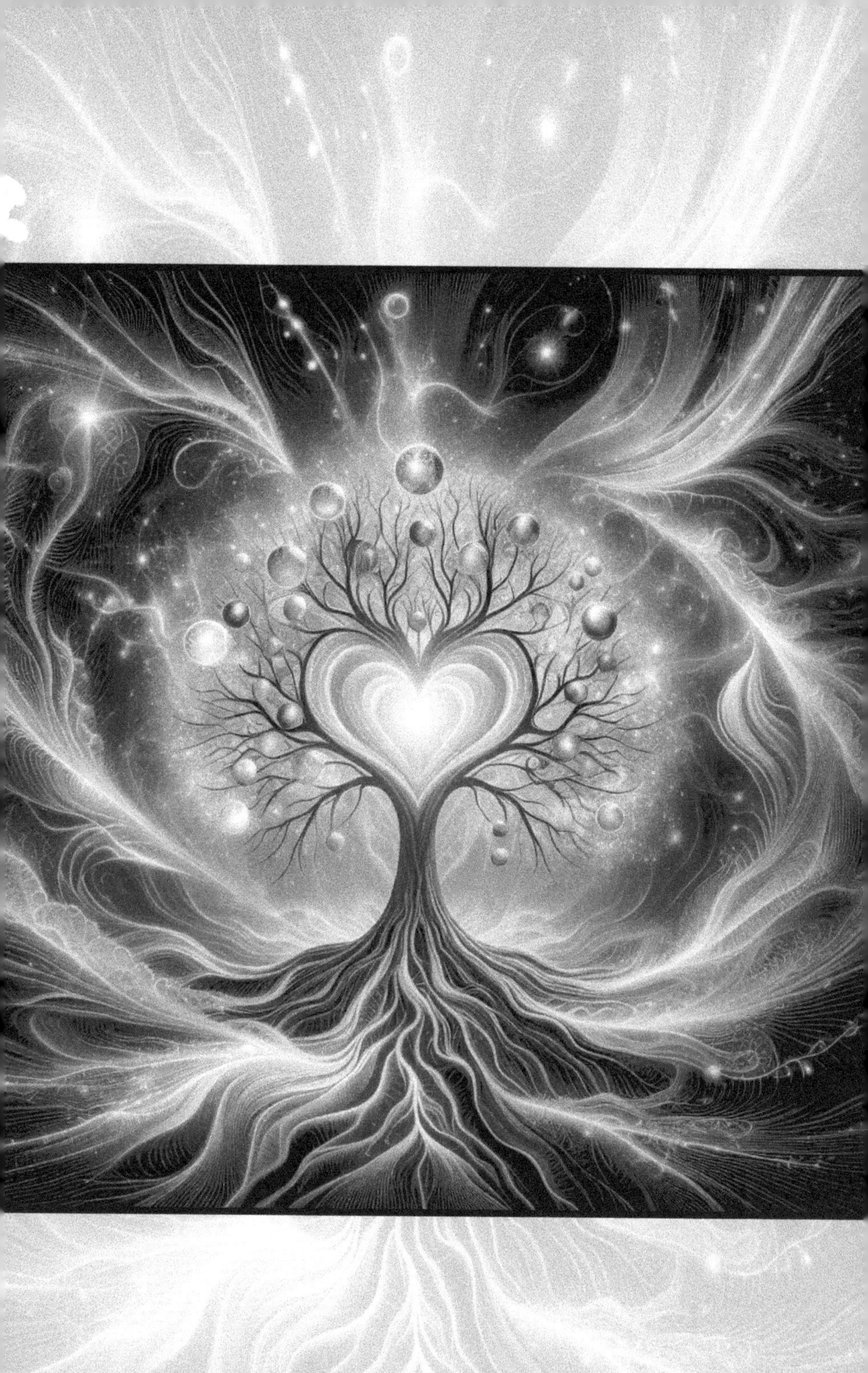

Chapter 12

Free And Clear Spaces—The How-To's

When the time comes to *clearing the space* in a relationship, there are certain elements we can use to create a more conducive environment and facilitate the process.

1. Choose a space with minimal distractions. When two people agree to sit and do a *clearing*, it is important to have as few distractions as possible. It is difficult enough to manage our emotional experience, attempt to communicate clearly without blame, monitor our past triggers, and remain present with our partner. Distractions, such as loud music or noise; interruptions from others; cell phone notifications; kids or pets running around; or even visual stimuli; compromise our focus to varying degrees which results in less attention and energy for our intentions.

2. How are you feeling physically? Anything that requires our attention and energy creates a deficit in the attention and energy available to us for clearing the space. So, if you or your partner have pain or illness, feel tired or sleepy, or are inebriated, this will limit your attention and zap your energy. Your lack of presence will make it more difficult to accomplish your intentions. Make sure you both feel generally well and are present and alert so that you have as much awareness for the process as possible.

3. Did anything happen during the day that has captured your thoughts? Are you experiencing worries about the near future? Begin by taking a few deep breaths, let go of any thoughts of the past and worries about the future and bring as much attention to the present moment as possible. This will be an ongoing task since we can often find ourselves thinking about what we are going to say in response. This can cause us to go into the future and lose presence with what the other is communicating.

4. Now that you are present, there are a couple of things to remember. First and foremost, you are a team. You have both made the choice to create a relationship and are choosing to participate in each other's Life process, which includes healing your pasts. You are allies, not enemies! When your partner is clearing their resentments, remember they are sharing their inner experiences and perceptions. All experiences and viewpoints are valid; we see things in our own unique way. Also, most of our resentments are connected to our past resentments and disappointments, so in most cases our partner is speaking to someone in their past— you are simply a trigger. Remembering this will help you to not take things as personally.

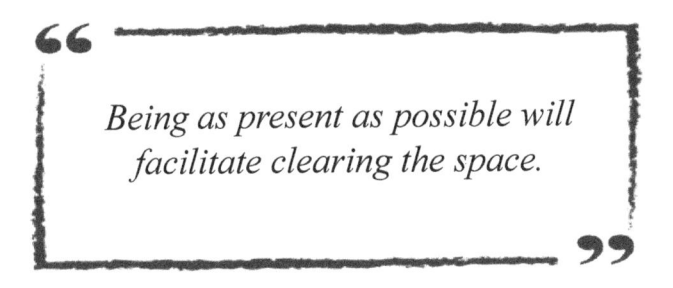

> *Being as present as possible will facilitate clearing the space.*

Now let's begin a clearing between Abbie and Ben. They have decided to have Abbie begin. While clearing her resentments, Abbie does the best she can to take responsibility for her emotions and feelings. For example, she says, "When you said you didn't want to talk about unimportant stuff, I felt disregarded, like what was important to me was insignificant. It caused me to feel like I am not important to you."

That approach takes more responsibility than, "When you said you didn't want to talk about unimportant stuff, you made me feel insignificant. You make me feel like I'm not good enough for you."

In reality, no one can make us feel anything. It all depends on how *we* choose to interpret or filter something that causes us to feel certain ways. That depends on us and us alone. Abbie needs to communicate the best she can taking ownership and not blaming Ben for her feelings and emotions. Remember, we are powerless as long as we blame anything or anyone outside of ourselves for our reality.

In the process of Abbie giving voice to her resentments, it is crucial that Ben not defend any of her points of contention. If Ben defends any of Abbie's communications, that defense invalidates Abbie's perceptions and experiences. What his defense inadvertently says is, "You're looking at it the wrong way," or "You are incorrect in your perceptions." In other words, you are wrong for feeling what you are feeling. Any amount of defense will close the space to Abbie's way of seeing things and will not allow the resentment's energy to be released.

Abbie's perceptions will, most likely, not be the same as Ben's. What makes any one person's perceptions more valid than another's? Nothing! It is vital that Ben allow Abbie to talk uninterrupted. The only words that Ben is permitted to say are "OK," or "I hear you," or any other kind of acknowledgement that lets Abbie know he is receiving her communications. That is all!

Ben should also notice any reactivity that may be triggered in him by Abbie's clearing. At the same time, actively trying to see things from Abbie's perspective by asking himself,

"If I were in her place, could I have also perceived it the same way?" Ben needs to allow Abbie to continue to speak until she feels she has nothing more to say. In essence, Ben becomes a space in which Abbie can share her inner reality, due to her perceptions.

> *Any kind of defense, no matter how small, closes the space and the person clearing feels their communication is not received.*

Once Abbie is finished sharing, Ben starts to communicate his inner experiences. These will include his perspective of his side of the experience. This will give Abbie insight as to why he acted or said the things he did. Ben will also share his resentments as Abbie becomes a space for Ben to share his reality. Abbie will also do her best to put herself in Ben's place to try to understand his perspective.

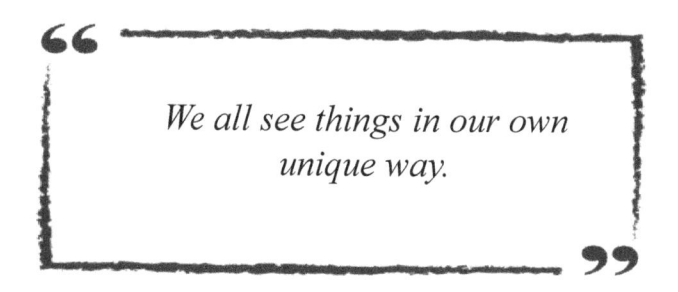

> *We all see things in our own unique way.*

Abbie and Ben may take a few turns at sharing, as new feelings or emotions may be triggered by each other's clearing. Things might get heavy during the process, especially in the beginning and middle phases. However, Abbie and Ben will feel increasingly lighter as the process continues.

Here is the bottom line—our judgments, expectations, demands and resentments of those we are in relationship with take energy to hold on to. Once we clear these and release them, it frees that energy for Love. It is common to feel a sense of renewed Love and connection after a clearing. This process also serves us to become more expanded in our experience of Life.

To the degree that we are triggered in our past pain and trauma, we will become unconscious. Consciousness is the difference between an expression and a reaction. As a result, we often say things that may be hurtful to others. Our intentions are probably not to hurt or cause pain to another, but in our unconscious reactions we often do. It is a good practice to take a moment, whenever possible, to pause, take a breath and refrain from saying the first hurtful thing that comes up.

I have come up with a technique that works well for me when I feel emotionally baited. If I am talking on the phone with someone who is obviously pushing my buttons and looking for a fight, I simply say, "I'm going to have to call you back." It would be so easy for my past self to engage in a conflict with this person who knows how to hook my reactivity. We all know many people who have this ability. We also possess the ability to trigger others; knowing exactly what will get them to take the bait and get hooked onto our emotional fishing rod. By telling the person on the other line that we need to call them back, we buy ourselves some time to reflect.

When we get some distance from the hook that holds an enticing, aromatic favorite-flavored appetizer, we can reflect a bit more objectively. Based on our highest good, we make our choice of how to respond. *We* decide what we will allow to enter our sacred space of Self, never blaming the person for our own triggers. We also might realize that something has likely happened to them before our conversation that has caused them to lash out and engage in some kind of conflict.

When we call back, we respond as authentically as possible, including compassion for their difficulty; whatever that may be; and offer any service we are willing to give to assist the other in clearing their conflict. We do not owe this person our participation in conflict. We do not owe them the service of assistance. *We* get to choose what and how we are willing to provide if anything at all. Buying ourselves time works miracles, because we no longer are pressured to give reactions that come from our unconscious triggers. We give ourselves the permission to take the time to resource our greater Self and let our responses come from that deeper, broader place within us.

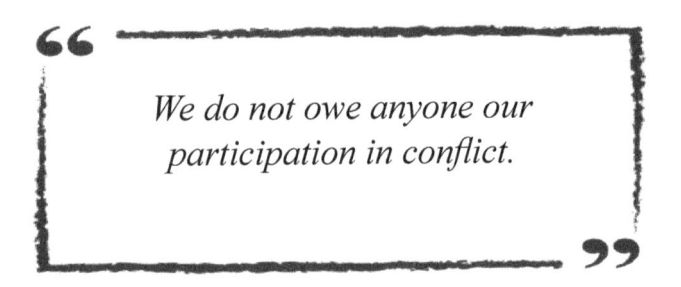

> *We do not owe anyone our participation in conflict.*

We each have a certain capacity to hold Love, depending on how much of that potential is taken up by reactivity, unconscious attitudes, coping mechanisms, judgments, expectations and demands of others. Our physical, emotional and mental health also have a bearing on this capacity. All of these elements take energy to hold on to, and that energy will be unavailable for us to hold Love. That is why the teaching of forgiveness is so significant. The teaching that we forgive, not for the other person, but rather for ourselves. If we are holding on to resentment, judgement, hostility or even hate, it will block our ability to experience Love.

With that in mind, create a free and clear space in your relationships; then do periodic relational maintenance tokeep that space as clear as possible.

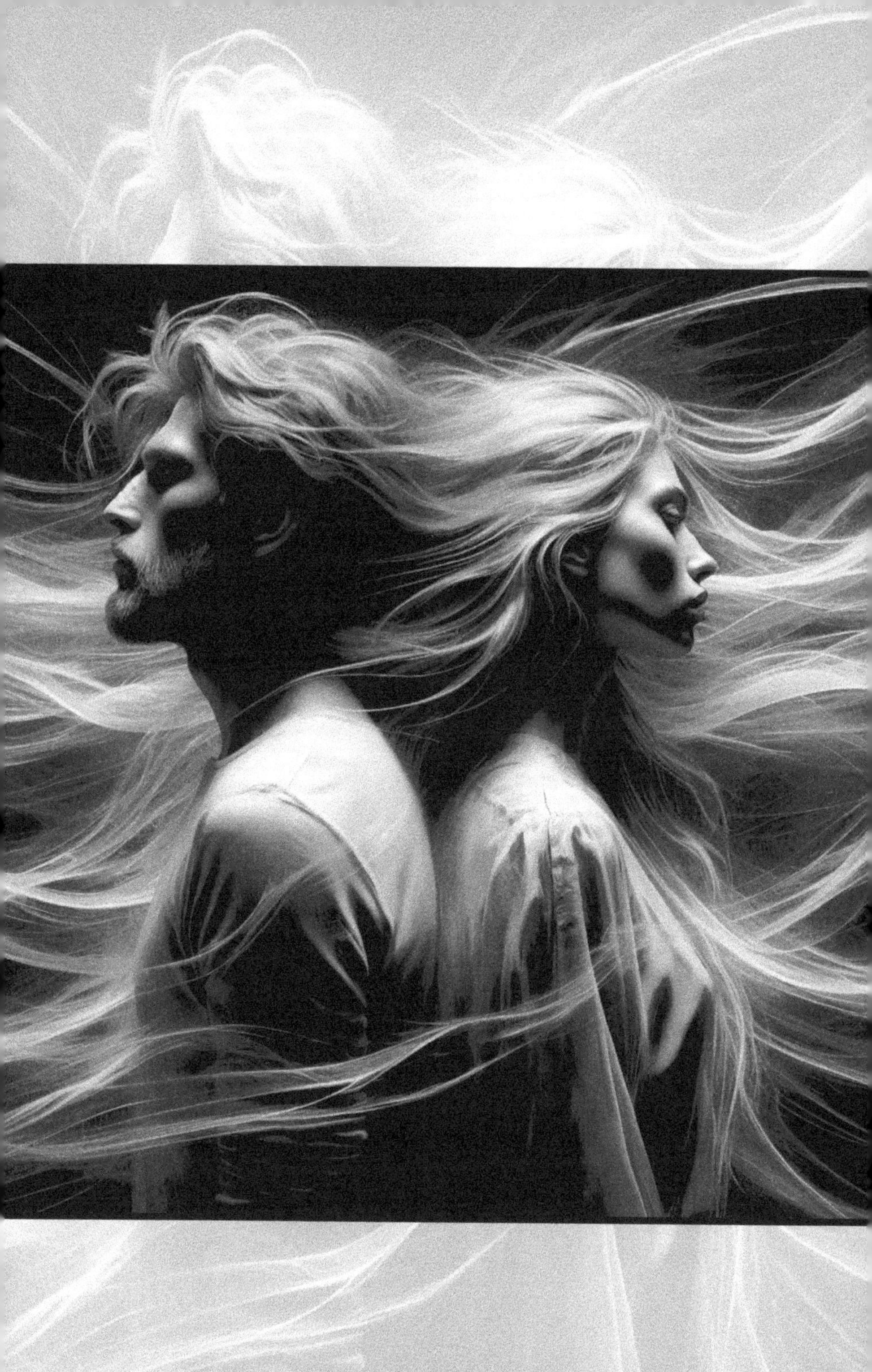

Chapter 13

Divine What? Spiritual Who?

Everything in Life is a *practice*. That means once we make the choice to walk on a path of being more conscious, we will continually need to ask ourselves the question, "How does this serve my conscious evolution?" Until we become established in Love, we will continue to experience a regressive pull toward fear and fearful ways of being. We will re-experience confusion, reactivity, defensiveness, closing down, etc. When you find yourself stuck in your mind and muddled by judgments, expectations, demands and resentments of others and cannot correct your thinking, ask yourself this question: "Does this behavior, attitude, reactivity, etc., serve my spiritual evolution?" Asking this question reminds us of the choice we have made to seek consciousness and the commitment to our greater Selves that goes hand in hand. If we live in the question, eventually we will become the answer and remember who we are.

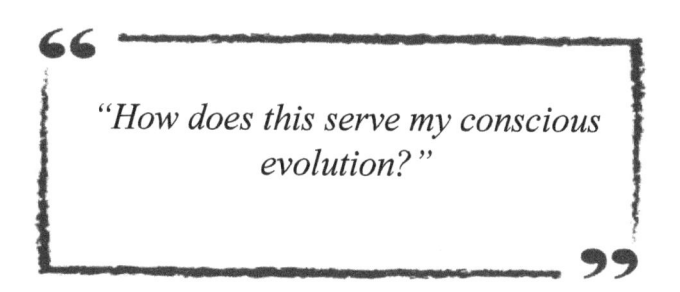

> "How does this serve my conscious evolution?"

Sure, we may have times of negativity and crisis; in fact, that is likely a certainty rather than a probability. And sometimes we may not be able to pull ourselves out of it. During those times, be kind to yourself. I remember my teacher often saying, "You guys, be good to yourselves, comfort yourselves. The world beats us up enough. It doesn't need our help."

None of us is a perfect being, we are all in the *process of becoming*. And, even when we get to where we long to be, there will be a further process of becoming. My teacher called it the divine impulse, and it is encoded in our DNA. It is in our very basic structure of Life to evolve, though we all evolve in our own way and at our own speed.

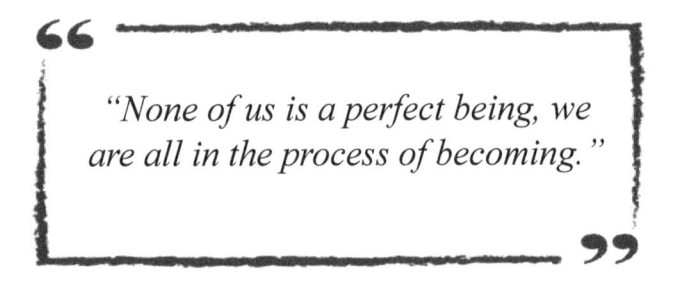

> *"None of us is a perfect being, we are all in the process of becoming."*

Something else that is encoded in our DNA is the desire to help others along the way. This can be kind of tricky at times, believe me. Sometimes we give advice, counseling, mentoring or assistance to people who never asked for help. Often, I have had the best intentions to help others and have had it explode in my face. We need to become very perceptive in how open other people are to their own spiritual growth. Some people have chosen to be exactly where they are and do not want to change. No matter how fervently we wish for others to be more evolved, we cannot make it come true; it is out of our hands. It is their choice to make change happen, or not, which is perfect for their process. Eventually, we will come to recognize the people who were somehow guided to find us, because we are able to serve them in some way. These are the people who we are meant to serve.

> *"Some people have chosen to be exactly where they are and do not want to change."*

So how do we support the divine impulse in others? Consider this example. About one-and-a-half years ago I met Isaac. He confessed to me that he didn't know how to swim. I was lucky enough to learn how to swim at a very young age and have always loved the water. I knew this was not the case for Isaac, who always had an underlying dread of the water, so much so that he never even entered a pool at the shallow end.

One of my great enjoyments is to kayak on a paddle board out on Biscayne Bay. When I shared this with Isaac, he said,

"Really, you do that? Maybe I'll do that with you one day." I responded with a simple, "OK." Although I went out a couple of times a week, he never mentioned the possibility of joining me. That went on for months until one day, out of the blue, he said, "Hey, if you go out today, I want to go with you."

"Really?" I asked.

"Yes" he replied. I knew that "Yes" was his divine impulse talking. In the months that had passed, I'd never pressured him or even mentioned the possibility of him joining me. I knew he must have had a really strong desire because his request felt energized. It did not feel like a frivolous notion. I also knew that it would be a huge confrontation for him, even though he would be wearing a life jacket and a paddle board, as I explained, is very difficult to tip over since they are totally flat and very wide.

As we walked to the launching point; below a bridge with a concrete ledge just inches above the water; I explained the logistics of paddling and maneuvering the paddle board. My style is to sit on the paddle board with a double kayak paddle and have a relaxing time for a couple of hours, rather than to make it a rigorous and intense shorter workout.

I could tell his apprehension was building as we finished

inflating the boards. I told him, "We will get you on your board first so you feel stable, and I will follow." As soon as he sat on the board, he panicked. The reality had hit him that he was on an unstable surface and was at eye level with small but confrontive waves. He said, "I can't do this. No."

Instinctively, I knew his "No" was his fearful ego stopping him in his tracks, rejecting an experience outside his comfort zone and causing him to freeze. We have all had this kind of experience before, when we want to feel the joy and freedom of a particular experience but our fear does not allow it. So many times, in our past, fear has dominated our actions and kept us locked in a prison of immobility and self-doubt. I had no intention of allowing his fear to deprive him from experiencing the joy and freedom of Biscayne Bay on a paddle board. I was determined to serve the "Yes" of his greater Self.

So I said, "OK, close your eyes and take a breath. I am here with you and will not let anything happen to you. You are safe, your life jacket will always keep you afloat, and it's not easy to tip the board over even if you try. Relax and know you will be OK."

After a few minutes he opened his eyes, and Isaac was back. His divine impulse was present again. We had an amazing time out on the bay, and he was so grateful to have had the experience. Had I not supported and served his divine impulse and allowed his "No" to take over and win, he would have felt awful about himself for quite a while. He would have felt as though he had failed himself because he really wanted to have the experience. I did not convince him or coerce him. I simply supported his desire for expansion, and he allowed me to support him. It was ultimately his choice, and he made it for himself.

That's how I choose to help people now. I never push or try to convince anyone to do something that is unfamiliar to them. However, if they want to experience something new, then I will serve their yearning to expand. I have realized that my past is full of times that I let myself down and allowed my fear to stop me from doing something I was drawn to do. All of us experience fear of the unknown or whatever is out of our comfort zone. The question is, are we going to have the fear and do it anyway? I know I've had enough of letting my fear make choices for me. Have you?

I support your divine impulse for conscious evolution. I challenge you to change your "No" to a "Yes" and dive into the depths of your being. Into the unknown spaces where we meet all the different parts of ourselves and invite them to the party.

Are you ready for the adventure of Self?

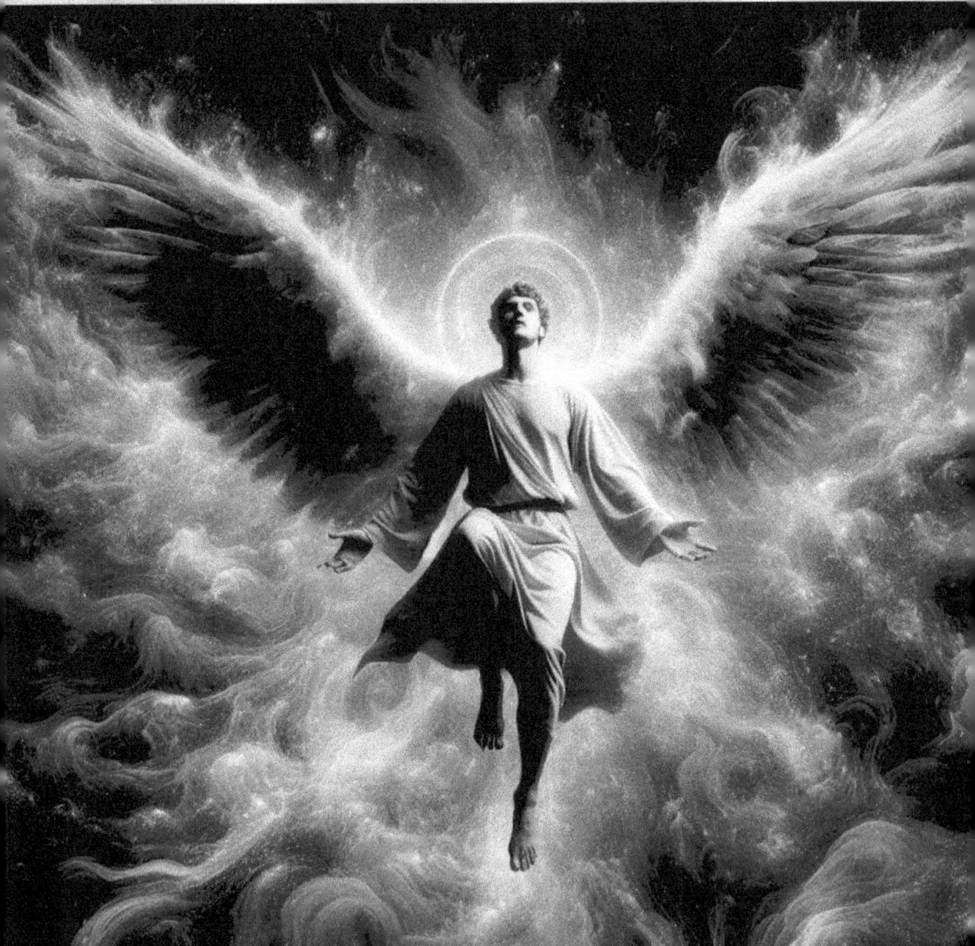

Appendix

There are a couple of points that I want to include in this work that did not find their way into any particular chapter, so I have included them here.

The first point has to do with conversation or gossip. We all know when we are participating with the energy of gossip. It is usually derogatory and most likely divulges information that is not ours to divulge. At other times, we use examples of other people's lives to share a lesson or broaden a perspective. This is delivered and communicated with a whole other energy and intention. This issue gets a little grayer in romantic relationships. In that situation, where do we draw the line as to what is ours to talk about?

In my first relationship (Jordy, if you recall), Jordy said to me one day, "I don't want you to talk to Marcy about everything that happens in our relationship."

I'll never forget my response: "I'm the type of person who needs to talk about my experiences. If I'm confused or need to vent, talking to someone about it gets everything out of my head and puts it out there. That gives me a clearer perspective and helps me understand things better. If you don't need to do this for yourself, I get it, but if I have an experience with you,

I am part of that experience and I have the right to talk about it, if I need to. I will not, however, talk about anything that has to do with you alone. Those things are not mine to share." He understood and never mentioned it again.

This issue has come up quite a few times in counseling when one partner is private and keeps things to themselves and the other is a communicator and has the need to be open and talk about their thoughts and feelings. When I share this story with them, it gives them insight into their partner and helps them to feel more relaxed about both responses to the issue.

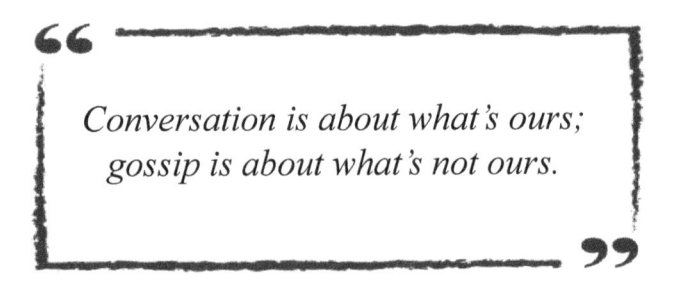

> *Conversation is about what's ours; gossip is about what's not ours.*

The **second point** is that personal freedom is created by establishing clear boundaries. We are all unique expressions of Life in this world. We have our own preferences, abilities, strengths, and challenges. As we discover and become familiar with our authentic Selves, we will need to create boundaries in which our uniqueness has a space to exist. I'll give you an example of this in my own Life.

As long as I can remember, I have been a night owl. My mom always had a difficult time trying to get me to bed before eleven p.m., and it was very difficult to wake me in the morning. Later when I worked a nine-to-five job, I personally found it difficult to get my body out of bed. As a result, I was late more often than my co-workers. When I became self-employed, my particular circadian rhythm started to express itself and my natural sleep cycle of 4:30 a.m. to 12:30 p.m. had the space to exist.

Something else happens to me while I sleep. I sleep so deeply; hence the difficulty in waking up; that I have a long process of returning to this physical reality. I've realized over the years, that in this state my mind does not connect sufficiently to allow me to express my thoughts clearly. It takes me about one to one-and-a-half hours after waking before I feel like I am fully here in the physical realm.

I realize that I am not like most people or at least how most people need to live their lives to fulfill their job requirements. I know that when I am waking up most people are already having lunch; they have been awake for five, six or seven hours and are in fifth gear. If I were to speak with any of those early risers when I am just waking, we would basically be in different time zones. We would not be able to connect easily; I would not do a good job at coherent speech. I have also realized that if I am asked a question that requires consideration or planning during this time, it causes me stress. So, I have created a clear boundary for myself. I will not answer the phone until a certain time. I am willing to answer texts or emails, but my responses tend to be brief. This clear boundary gives me the space to express who and how I am—which is personal freedom.

We all need to consider the space around us as our sacred space of Self. Only we decide who or what will enter that space. Imagine that you live in a building with five-hundred units. If you leave your apartment door open, others may walk in. If you close the door others will have to knock, allowing you to choose whether to let them in or not. It is the same with personal boundaries. If you have none, others will disregard your sacred space. If your boundaries are clear, then you can decide who you let into that sacred space. Most of us have grown up in a world with blatant disregard to the boundaries of others, as well as our own. There is nothing selfish in taking care of your own physical, emotional, mental and spiritual well-being. Most of us have been conditioned to feel an obligation toward the expectations of others—their judgments and demands of us—and if we do not feel obligated to comply, we should feel guilty about it.

It is time to drop this misconception. If we take care of, Love and honor ourselves, we will be healthier and more available to serve others.

> *"We all need to consider the space around us as our sacred space of Self."*

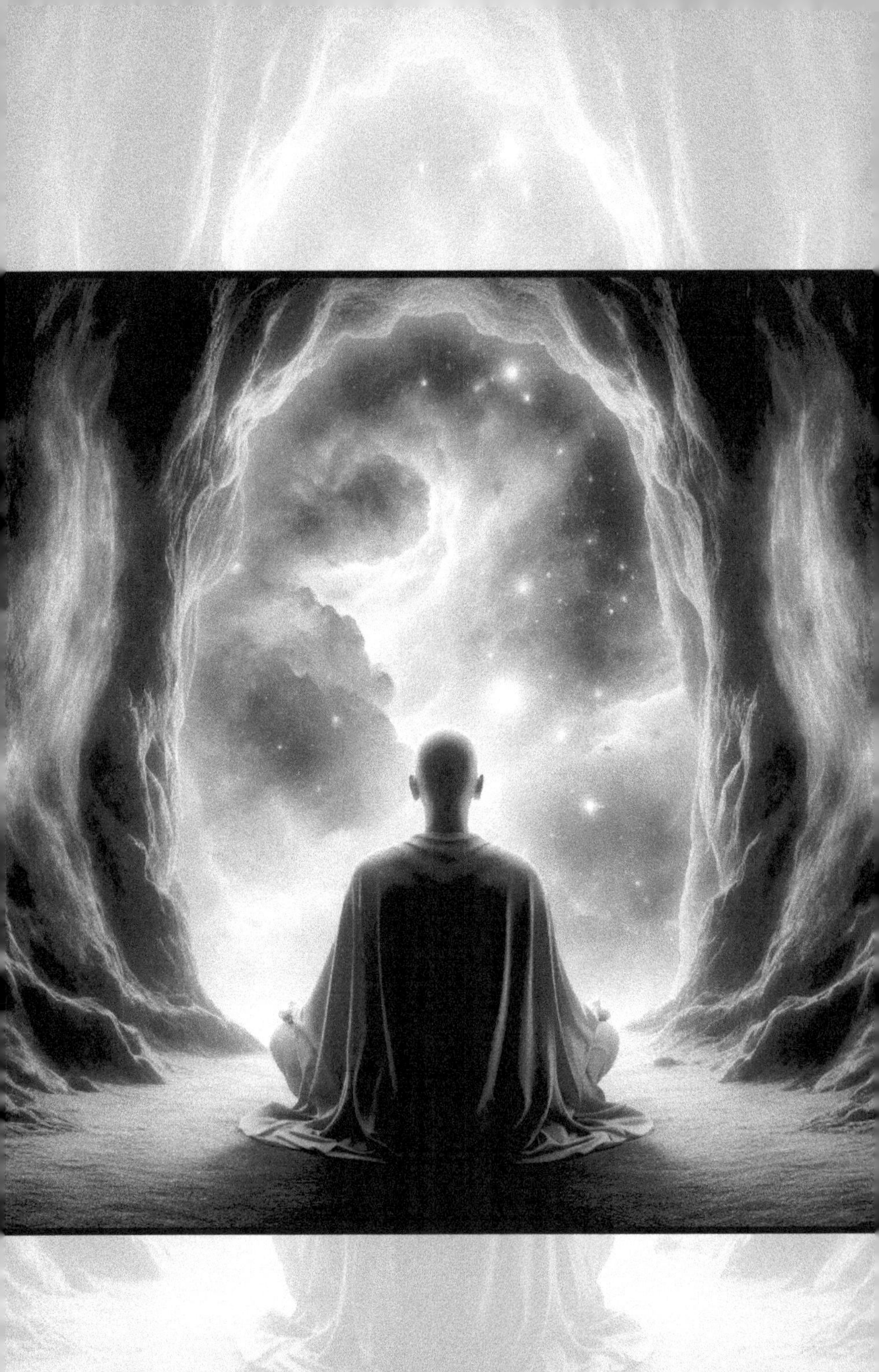

About The Author

Lohan Bruguera is a healer and breath-worker; Life coach and licensed massage therapist; and has touched many lives, not only physically, but emotionally, mentally, and spiritually. Lohan began his search for deeper meaning as a young adult, exploring multiple paths and philosophies. His profound spiritual process began in 1990, when he met his spiritual teacher, Isana Mada Grace Dhyana.

Lohan cultivates his abilities through an inner process, providing his clients with a safe space for healing. By sharing his teachings of authenticity and self-expression, he helps others achieve a broader perspective. With in-depth knowledge, wisdom, and experience, he asks the questions to encourage us to look deeper and live expansively.

Lohan believes our education system focuses on creating

employees, not the basics of being human: i.e., how to communicate, process emotions, contribute to sane relationships, and express ourselves authentically. This revelation led him to share his heart-centered methods.

Lohan hopes humanity can escape our psychological confinement and become free.

Lohan Bruguera lives in Miami, Florida with his two dogs.

He would love to hear from you. Connect with him here: https://linktr.ee/lohanbruguera

TRUE AUTHENTICITY PRESS

Maia would often say in front of groups of awakening ones: *"I don't know what your Truth is, but I know when you are not being your truth. And we can all feel it."* In other words; We connect to a person when they are coming from their authentic sense of self and we do not connect to someone who is not. We intuitively know when someone is expressing who they truly are.

On our way towards our most authentic self, it is helpful to know what qualities are most intrinsic in an authentic person. These are general qualities which will help you define what you need to improve on.

I invite you to take your free Authenticity Quotient test by scanning the QR code or using the link below.

https://uncoveryourauthenticity.com/english-book/

My next book will be: Authenticity Quotient: What is your AQ?

Printed in the USA
CPSIA information can be obtained
at www.ICGtesting.com
CBHW051750181024
16042CB00034B/1180